Manhattan Review®

Test Prep & Admissions Consulting

Turbocharge Your Career:
Smart Business Talk

2nd Edition (December 16th, 2011)

☐ *Expression by Keyword & Sport*

☐ *Useful Idioms & Euphemisms*

☐ *Workplace Slang & Idioms*

- *Corporate Hierarchy*
- *Performance Review*
- *Project Management*
- *Meetings and Conference Calls*
- *Hiring, Firing and Downsizing*
- *Negotiation & Conflict Resolutions*

☐ *Grammar Review & Specifics*

- *Use of Articles*
- *Use of Prepositions*

☐ *Presentational Skills*

☐ *Accent Reduction*

☐ *Cultural Sensitivity and Etiquette*

www.manhattanreview.com

Copyright and Terms of Use

10-Digit International Standard Book Number: (ISBN: 1629260118)
13-Digit International Standard Book Number: (ISBN: 978-1-62926-011-2)

Last updated on December 16, 2011.

Manhattan Review, 275 Madison Avenue, Suite 424, New York, NY 10016.

Phone: +1 (212) 316-2000. E-Mail: info@manhattanreview.com. Web: www.manhattanreview.com

About the Turbocharge Your Career Series

Smart Business Talk part of Manhattan Review's Turbocharge Your Career series. These insightful career instruction guides are designed for young professionals at all levels to improve their communication skills and functional knowledge within a short time period. They prove to be particularly helpful for students who have also taken corresponding Management Training courses with us.

√   **Smart Business Talk [2nd Edition]** (ISBN: 978-1-62926-011-2)
☐   **Negotiation & Decision Making [2nd Edition]** (ISBN: 978-1-62926-012-9)

About the Company

Manhattan Review's origin can be traced directly to an Ivy-League MBA classroom in 1999. While lecturing on advanced quantitative subjects to MBAs at Columbia Business School in New York City, Prof. Dr. Joern Meissner was asked by his students to assist their friends, who were frustrated with conventional GMAT preparation options. He started to create original lectures that focused on presenting the GMAT content in a coherent and concise manner rather than a download of voluminous basic knowledge interspersed with so-called "tricks." The new approach immediately proved highly popular with GMAT students, inspiring the birth of Manhattan Review. Over the past 15+ years, Manhattan Review has grown into a multi-national firm, focusing on GMAT, GRE, LSAT, SAT, and TOEFL test prep and tutoring, along with business school, graduate school and college admissions consulting, application advisory and essay editing services.

About the Founder

Professor Joern Meissner, the founder and chairman of Manhattan Review has over twenty-five years of teaching experience in undergraduate and graduate programs at prestigious business schools in the USA, UK and Germany. He created the original lectures, which are constantly updated by the Manhattan Review Team to reflect the evolving nature of the GMAT GRE, LSAT, SAT, and TOEFL test prep and private tutoring. Professor Meissner received his Ph.D. in Management Science from Graduate School of Business at Columbia University (Columbia Business School) in New York City and is a recognized authority in the area of Supply Chain Management (SCM), Dynamic Pricing and Revenue Management. Currently, he holds the position of Full Professor of Supply Chain Management and Pricing Strategy at Kuehne Logistics University in Hamburg, Germany. Professor Meissner is a passionate and enthusiastic teacher. He believes that grasping an idea is only half of the fun; conveying it to others makes it whole. At his previous position at Lancaster University Management School, he taught the MBA Core course in Operations Management and originated three new MBA Electives: Advanced Decision Models, Supply Chain Management, and Revenue Management. He has also lectured at the University of Hamburg, the Leipzig Graduate School of Management (HHL), and the University of Mannheim. Professor Meissner offers a variety of Executive Education courses aimed at business professionals, managers, leaders, and executives who strive for professional and personal growth. He frequently advises companies ranging from Fortune 500 companies to emerging start-ups on various issues related to his research expertise. Please visit his academic homepage www.meiss.com for further information.

International Phone Numbers & Official Manhattan Review Websites

Manhattan Headquarters	+1-212-316-2000	www.manhattanreview.com
USA & Canada	+1-800-246-4600	www.manhattanreview.com
Australia	+61-3-9001-6618	www.manhattanreview.com
Austria	+43-720-115-549	www.review.at
Belgium	+32-2-808-5163	www.manhattanreview.be
China	+1-212-316-2000	www.manhattanreview.cn
Czech Republic	+1-212-316-2000	www.review.cz
France	+33-1-8488-4204	www.review.fr
Germany	+49-89-3803-8856	www.review.de
Greece	+1-212-316-2000	www.review.com.gr
Hong Kong	+852-5808-2704	www.review.hk
Hungary	+1-212-316-2000	www.review.co.hu
India	+1-212-316-2000	www.review.in
Indonesia	+1-212-316-2000	www.manhattanreview.com
Ireland	+1-212-316-2000	www.gmat.ie
Italy	+39-06-9338-7617	www.manhattanreview.it
Japan	+81-3-4589-5125	www.manhattanreview.jp
Malaysia	+1-212-316-2000	www.manhattanreview.com
Netherlands	+31-20-808-4399	www.manhattanreview.nl
Philippines	+1-212-316-2000	www.review.ph
Poland	+1-212-316-2000	www.review.pl
Portugal	+1-212-316-2000	www.review.pt
Russia	+1-212-316-2000	www.manhattanreview.ru
Singapore	+65-3158-2571	www.gmat.sg
South Africa	+1-212-316-2000	www.manhattanreview.co.za
South Korea	+1-212-316-2000	www.manhattanreview.kr
Sweden	+1-212-316-2000	www.gmat.se
Spain	+34-911-876-504	www.review.es
Switzerland	+41-435-080-991	www.review.ch
Taiwan	+1-212-316-2000	www.gmat.tw
Thailand	+66-6-0003-5529	www.manhattanreview.com
United Arab Emirates	+1-212-316-2000	www.manhattanreview.ae
United Kingdom	+44-20-7060-9800	www.manhattanreview.co.uk
Rest of World	+1-212-316-2000	www.manhattanreview.com

Preface

Being able to use the everyday slang and idioms encountered in a typical business setting can make a big difference when you communicate with your English-speaking colleagues or friends. If someone tells you that you might be "called on the carpet" by the department head, do you know what's coming? When someone asks for your opinion, maybe you just want to offer your "two cents" as a valuable team player, not an over-bearing micromanager. If you don't want to keep arguing about minor issues, it's time for you to stop "splitting hairs." The good news is you will get plenty of these interesting expressions in just a few minutes. This handy book will walk you through phrases such as being "behind the eight ball", "pushing the envelope", and many more. You'll get clear explanations and examples of how to use them, allowing you to put them to use immediately.

While we are enjoying playing with slang and idioms, let's ask ourselves what we are trying to achieve by mastering these expressions. There are some fast and easy conclusions.

First, unnecessary misunderstanding and confusion can be minimized. If a colleague makes a complaint to you, you'll understand what that person means immediately. Moreover, if a client uses these informal expressions on an important professional occasion, you will "get a handle on" the feelings and connotations expressed within a split second. As a result, you are in a much more informed position to make your response, and you'll be able to leave a lasting impression with your team members.

Second, professional productivity and camaraderie can be increased. You'll have a more pleasant work environment and better team chemistry. You won't have to pretend you understand everything perfectly in a meeting, when actually you are quite confused.

Lastly, you will enjoy the vividness and efficiency of the English language on a daily basis. Language has many layers, and it is very satisfying to travel beneath the surface. These colloquial expressions have been developed through time, traveling many interesting paths within various contexts. It is amazing how few words can mean so much.

On a separate note, English has a great number of synonyms. Being able to choose a word precisely based on the context will help you say what you really mean, and say what you intend to make others hear. To avoid any fuzzy or mistaken impressions, it is absolutely necessary to distinguish between words of similar, but not identical, meaning.

To master all the expressions and synonyms quickly and effectively, start to use them today. Try the following exercises: paraphrasing, combining various phrases together in a short story, comparing the similarity of and the difference in both meaning and connotation between phrases, and filling in a blank sentence by blocking the featured expression.

To further aid your English fluency, we have included additional sections on grammar, accent reduction, presentational skills, and cultural awareness.

Your efforts will soon be rewarded, and we are happy to help during this process!

Contents

Chapter 1

Useful Common Idioms

1.1 A – G

Ace in the hole (to have/get an)
Meaning: A hidden advantage one has in order to control a situation
Example: He got an *ace in the hole*. His contacts in the company told him all the recent personnel changes in the group before his interview the next day.

Add insult to injury
Meaning: To make an unfavorable situation even worse
Example: Not only did she lose her job when Enron collapsed, but to *add insult to injury,* she also lost her pension.

Against the grain (to go)
Meaning: To act directly to the contrary of common practices
Example: The new CEO's lack of a graduate education went totally *against the grain* of the chairman's usual practice of hiring experienced MBAs from McKinsey.

Ahead of the game
Meaning: In advance of an original schedule or a peer group
Example: At the weekly meeting, our manager announced that we should all be looking for new clients. I was *ahead of the game* because I had already been calling various companies for weeks.

All in a day's work
Meaning: Referring to the normal activities one completes in a typical day
Example: For Lisa, an executive assistant, taking careful notes at the meetings was *all in a day's work*.

All things to all men
Meaning: Doing so much extra work that the tasks are usually impossible to complete
Example: The building manager was constantly busy helping all the tenants; it was clear he was trying to be *all things to all men*, but this unproductive approach resulted in more complaints.

As tough/hard as nails
Meaning: Strong-minded, not displaying emotions
Example: My boss is **as tough as nails**. However, he does his job well.

At arm's length
Meaning: Cautiously keeping someone or something at a distance from oneself
Example: The young project manager tried to keep Bob, the veteran in the group, **at arm's length** because she thought he was trying to undercut her authority.

At each other's throats
Meaning: When two people are in a serious argument or conflict with each other
Example: The two bosses were **at each other's throats** for weeks over the questionable decision one of them made for the company.

At first blush
Meaning: Upon first considering or seeing something
Example: **At first blush**, the advertising campaign seemed brilliant. Unfortunately, it turned out to be a complete failure in the end.

At one's wit's end
Meaning: Someone's breaking point due to frustration
Example: The boss was **at wit's end** with the employee who never understood his directions.

At sixes and sevens (British English)
Meaning: To be in a state of confusion
Example: The business school grad was **at sixes and sevens** over which job to accept.

At the drop of a hat
Meaning: To react immediately
Example: If I told him that I got him tickets at center court for the basketball game, he'd leave the office **at the drop of a hat** no matter how much work he had to do.

Average Joe
Meaning: An average person (male)
Example: This firm doesn't hire just any **average Joe**. The employees here are very distinguished and well rounded.

Babe in the woods
Meaning: A naive or innocent person
Example: The young consultant, a new addition to the company, was a **babe in the woods** compared to his experienced colleagues.

Back to square one (to go)
Meaning: To return to the first stage; return to the beginning
Example: Once the manager showed him that his formulas were all wrong, he had to go **back to square one** and start all over again.

Backseat driver
Meaning: Someone who goes beyond their own authority to give advice
Example: Despite being new and having little knowledge about our current project, Bob decided to become the **backseat driver** during the meeting and suggest a totally new approach.

Bald/bold/bare-faced lie
Meaning: An untruthful response given without care about its believability
Example: When she returned to work after a two-day absence, she told our boss some **bare-faced lie** about being in the hospital even though we all saw her out at the bar the night before.

Ball of fire
Meaning: Referring to someone with lots of energy and stamina
Example: The reason the company grew so fast was the founder was such a **ball of fire**. He worked tirelessly day and night.

Bang for the buck
Meaning: The amount of satisfaction or value one receives relative to the price they paid
Example: When it was time to buy a new car, the businessman decided that the Corvette was going to give him the biggest **bang for the buck**.

Bang-up job
Meaning: A high accomplishment
Example: The agent did a **bang-up job** in putting together a presentation that persuaded the athlete to sign on with the firm.

Bark up the wrong tree
Meaning: When one tries to get help from someone who cannot or will not help them
Example: When he asked the manager for a raise he was **barking up the wrong tree**. It was the group head he needed to talk to.

Be on the same page
Meaning: Be in agreement, or at least with an understanding of one another
Example: Before our manager continued the meeting, he made sure we were all **on the same page** regarding our responsibilities for the project.

Bean counter
Meaning: Someone who focuses on trivial details
Example: We often did not complete our tasks because Jim was being such a **bean counter**.

Beating a dead horse

Meaning: To continue harping on something after the situation has already been resolved

Example: After we decided not to buy the stock for our fund, she continued to try to convince us to buy it. We told her to stop **beating a dead horse** already!

Behind the eight ball

Meaning: Stuck in a difficult situation; to be at a disadvantage

Example: She was **behind the eight ball** on the project because she missed the last three meetings and lacked crucial information.

Bend over backwards

Meaning: To go to great lengths to help someone else

Example: From setting up the interview to lobbying her boss, Julia **bent over backwards** to make sure her friend got hired.

Best foot forward (to put one's)

Meaning: Make a good impression by showing one's strengths

Example: When interviewing for a job, it is pretty obvious that you should try to put your **best foot forward**.

Between a rock and a hard place

Meaning: A situation with two outcomes, both of which are not good

Example: He found himself **between a rock and a hard place** when he realized that whatever decision he made would upset someone in the company.

Between the lines (to read/look)

Meaning: The deeper, implicit meaning of something

Example: If you read **between the lines**, you'll realize that the Q2 report is going to force us to make some personnel changes around here.

Big shoes to fill

Meaning: When there are high expectations for someone because whoever filled the role previously did such a good job

Example: It was unfortunate that the CEO chose to retire. He was doing such a great job. Whoever becomes CEO next is going to have **big shoes to fill**.

Birds of a feather flock together

Meaning: People with similar ideas and outlooks associate with one another

Example: Many who work in the financial sector share conservative fiscal views about our government. I guess that **birds of a feather flock together**.

Bite off more than one can chew

Meaning: To take on more than is possible to complete

Example: When he accepted the role of building manager in addition to his other job, he may have been **biting off more than he could chew**.

Bite the bullet

Meaning: To accept something undesirable in order to ultimately achieve a desired outcome

Example: If you want to make partner you're just going to have to **bite the bullet** and put in really long hours for the next couple years.

Blind alley (to go down a)

Meaning: A path that will result in futility

Example: You're going **down a blind alley** if you think that studying that company's history will tell you how it's going to fare in the future.

Blind leading the blind

Meaning: When one uninformed person advises another uninformed person

Example: When we were trying to find the building site in Baltimore, it was like **the blind leading the blind.** We had no clue where we were going.

Blow it

Meaning: To ruin a situation by making a bad decision

Example: We're on track to make fifty thousand dollars by day's end so don't **blow it** by trading any of that stock yet!

Blow/toot one's own horn

Meaning: To give praise to oneself

Example: Even though she has single-handedly made this company what it is today, she never **blows her own horn**. She is the most modest person I know.

Blow smoke

Meaning: To tell someone something with the deliberate intention of hiding the truth

Example: When the company's president told the employees that layoffs were not coming in the near future, he was merely **blowing smoke** since, just weeks later, 5,000 workers lost their jobs.

Blow the whistle on someone

Meaning: To expose bad actions with the hope of stopping them

Example: When he saw her taking money out of the cash register, he **blew the whistle on** her and told the manager.

Origin: Long ago crime scenes where the police blew their whistles to stop an offender.

Breathe down one's neck

Meaning: To hover over someone in a way that makes him/her uncomfortable

Example: Even though my boss wasn't in the office, I could feel him **breathing down my neck** to get the report finished. He called me every five minutes to check on my progress.

Bring it home

Meaning: Make something understandable to someone

Example: By using a sports analogy to explain teamwork in the office, my boss's explanation really **brought it home** for me.

Build a better mousetrap

Meaning: To come up with a more efficient remedy for a problem

Example: Instead of yelling across the entire office, why don't we just **build a better mousetrap** and get an intercom system?

Bull session (to have)

Meaning: A brainstorming meeting or conversation where those involved speak their minds and hash out potential ideas

Example: The office morale seems really low. Let's have a **bull session** to hear everyone's concerns and decide how to make a better atmosphere.

Burn one's bridges

Meaning: To make decisions that can't be changed in the future; to act in a way that means you will not be welcome to return in the future

Example: When the sports agent left the firm to start his own business, he **burned his bridges** with everyone who had helped him become successful.

Bury one's head in the sand

Meaning: To avoid unpleasant things by simply ignoring them

Example: Instead of **burying your head in the sand**, you should get out of your chair and go confess that you broke the copier.

Carry/have a chip on one's shoulder

Meaning: To continue to be upset about a past event; to hold a grudge

Example: He's still **carrying a chip on his shoulder** over the deal that fell through last week.

Carry the ball

Meaning: To take on the responsibility for doing something

Example: Our firm hired a very experienced economist to **carry the ball** and to help us compete for the big accounts.

Different strokes for different folks

Meaning: Everyone has their own ways of doing things, and their own preferences

Example: Did he really decide to decorate his office with pink polka-dotted wallpaper? I guess there are **different strokes for different folks**.

Divide and conquer

Meaning: To take on a challenge by breaking it down into smaller parts in order to be successful

Example: Our competitors are gaining on us. Let's **divide and conquer** by each of us going to their stores to see what they are doing differently from us.

Dog and pony show
Meaning: When something is exhibited with flourishing style and high attention to detail

Example: When I went to interview with that financial firm, they gave me the whole *dog and pony show* to try to sell me on joining their company.

Don't switch horses in midstream
Meaning: The thought that it is a mistake to change direction or to change who is in charge in the middle of some action

Example: Even though our CEO had lost the company money over the last year, the board decided not to *switch horses in midstream* with the hope that the CEO could fix his own mistakes.

Dose/taste of one's own medicine (to get or give)
Meaning: To be treated badly in the same way that you treated someone else earlier

Example: Bob was tired of Steve never helping him, so when Steve called Bob for help, Bob decided to give him a taste of his own medicine .

Dot the i's and cross the t's
Meaning: To be painstaking in one's attention to detail

Example: Before you agree to buy the building, make sure you *dot the "i's" and cross the "t's"* by having an inspector check out the shape that it's in.

Down (or up) one's alley
Meaning: To suit someone perfectly

Example: My brother's really good at math. Crunching numbers is right *up his alley.*

Synonym: One's cup of tea

Down the tubes
Meaning: Ruining something without hope of being able to repair it

Example: After she called him a horrible name, she pretty much threw that deal right *down the tubes*. There's no way that company is going to want to do business with us again.

Down to the wire
Meaning: Approaching a deadline

Example: It's getting *down to the wire* here. We need a decision on that stock before the market closes.

Drop the ball
Meaning: When one doesn't fulfill a responsibility they have been given

Example: Susan really *dropped the ball* on that project. I thought she said she had it under control, but I guess she didn't.

Dry run
Meaning: A practice try

Example: Before you go to your interview, let's do a *dry run* and practice your answers to these potential questions.

Earn one's stripes

Meaning: Outstanding performance of one's duties, typically earning them public recognition

Example: You have **earned your stripes** and I am going to give you a promotion and a raise.

Eat at someone

Meaning: When someone is deeply bothered by something

Example: I got in an argument with my boss and it has been **eating at me** all week-end.

Eat out of (the palm of) one's hand

Meaning: Possessing control over others

Example: My assistant has me **eating out of the palm of her hand.** I gave her two weeks off when she asked without even thinking twice about it.

Eleventh hour

Meaning: The final chance to achieve a goal

Example: Sarah always waits until the **eleventh hour** to turn in her business reports.

Fall on one's face

Meaning: To make a mistake in the presence of others

Example: He **fell on his face** one too many times in front of the boss. She fired him after the last mistake.

Fast talker

Meaning: Someone who talks in a clever way and convinces people of things that are not necessarily honest

Example: Tom's a real **fast talker**, so beware of anything he says.

Feather in one's cap

Meaning: An accomplishment

Example: Completing the sale of our largest property was a **feather in Gloria's cap.** She said she got a huge bonus at the end of last year because of it.

Fill/fit the bill

Meaning: To be what is needed

Example: After interviewing a dozen candidates, we decided to hire John. He **filled the bill** more than any of the other people we interviewed.

Fishing expedition

Meaning: An effort to find something worthwhile in spite of the fact that there are no specific aims at the start of the search

Example: The IRS launched an investigation into our accounting activities, but I feel like it's more of a **fishing expedition** than anything else.

Fly by the seat of one's pants

Meaning: To make decisions by feel or instinct, not following a specific plan

Example: He's really successful and much of the reason for his success comes from his impulsive decision-making. He definitely *flies by the seat of his pants!*

Related: *Play it by ear; wing it*

Fly off the handle

Meaning: To become very angry

Example: I wouldn't sit there and play computer games. If the boss sees you, he's going to *fly off the handle.*

Food for thought

Meaning: A new piece of information that needs time to be fully understood

Example: Our boss's motivational speeches leave us with *food for thought* about ways we could improve our efficiency.

For the birds

Meaning: Refers to something that is not appealing or worthwhile to someone

Example: I think our company's strategy for improving output is *for the birds.* Our current strategy works just fine!

From the horse's mouth

Meaning: From the original source

Example: It's not a rumor because we heard it straight *from the horse's mouth;* the CEO told us himself.

Fudge factor

Meaning: Room allowed for mistakes

Example: When I create a budget, I usually add five percent as a *fudge factor* to be safe.

Full plate

Meaning: To have a lot to complete

Example: I always see her running around like she has so much to do. She must have a *full plate.*

Gear up for something

Meaning: To mentally and/or physically prepare oneself for something

Example: I am getting all *geared up for* the GMAT exam. I have all the materials I need and I feel ready to take it on.

Get a grip

Meaning: Regain composure

Example: I know he made a mistake, but you should *get a grip* and calm down before you talk to him. He didn't forget to send those faxes intentionally.

Get back on one's feet
Meaning: After a difficult event that disrupts your life, you find a way to return to your usual habits and successes

Example: After Jane lost many of her possessions in the hurricane, it was very nice of her boss to help her **get back on her feet** by offering financial assistance.

Get down to the nitty-gritty
Meaning: To concentrate on the details

Example: Now that we know the basic layout of how we want the new offices to look, let's **get down to the nitty-gritty** and really decide specific details.

Get in on the act
Meaning: To join in on a situation that will bring you some kind of benefit

Example: After Google's stock price skyrocketed, everybody wanted to **get in on the act** and buy some of it with the hope that it would continue to rise.

Get in on the ground floor
Meaning: To involve oneself in a business or organization in its infancy, before it becomes successful

Example: Those of us who knew Google would be a success bought their stock early on and **got in on the ground floor**.

Get one's feet wet
Meaning: To join in and get experience

Example: We didn't want the new employee to just watch and learn. Instead, we wanted him to **get his feet wet** and learn by doing.

Get to first base
Meaning: To accomplish the first step

Example: The process of applying to business schools is a long one, but **getting to first base** requires you to fill out an application.

Gild the lily
Meaning: To add fake or superficial value or improvements to something that does not require improvement

Example: Everything in the report looks perfect. It's not necessary to go over it again. Anything you would add would just be **gilding the lily**.

Give one the brush-off
Meaning: To reject someone

Example: It's no fun being an intern. The bosses let us sit in on the meetings, but they always **give us the brush-off** whenever we try to offer our ideas.

Going like gangbusters
Meaning: Doing something with lots of excitement

Example: As soon as our doors opened, customers were **going like gangbusters** for the most wanted holiday gifts and gadgets.

Grin and bear it

Meaning: To tolerate a difficult situation without showing your displeasure because you have no other choice

Example: Even though he hated the idea of having to go to Alaska on a business trip, he had to **grin and bear it** in front of his boss.

1.2 H – N

Habit of mind

Meaning: Regular thought process

Example: Second guessing my own calculations is such a **habit of mind** for me. I made one small mistake a few years ago and ever since that time, I haven't trusted my own work.

Handwriting on the wall

Meaning: Indicates an obvious future result

Example: We all knew she was going to be fired sometime in the near future; the **handwriting was on the wall** since she stopped caring about getting to work on time.

Hang around

Meaning: Aimless loitering

Example: Even though he's supposed to leave work at 5 o'clock, I often see him **hanging around** the office well after 6.

Harp on a point

Meaning: To keep emphasizing something

Example: The boss continuously **harps on a point** until he's sure we all understand it.

Have a bone to pick

Meaning: When someone has a problem with someone else and wants to discuss it

Example: Can you come here for a minute? I have a **bone to pick** with you. Why in the world did you throw out those documents when you knew I hadn't seen them yet?

Have a good head on one's shoulders

Meaning: Someone who is sensible and aware

Example: Bob and our boss really get along well. I think she respects him because he **has a good head on his shoulders** and rarely makes bad decisions.

Have a leg up

Meaning: To have an advantage

Example: Graduates of prestigious business schools **have a leg up** on other job candidates who have less education.

Have a mind of one's own
Meaning: Someone who is able to make a decision without the influence of others
Example: When we interview potential employees, we always try to make sure they *have a mind of their own* and possess leadership qualities.

Heads up
Meaning: Aware of the situation
Example: When trading stock, you have to be *heads up* at all times and recognize when the best time is to buy or to sell.

High and dry
Meaning: Left helpless or stranded in a situation
Example: Though he had promised that he would assist me in the presentation, he left me *high and dry* when he did not even show up.

Hit the nail on the head
Meaning: Pinpoint a problem or situation with insights
Example: Carol *hit the nail on the head* when she suggested that the inadequate marketing budget was the reason for the recent profit decline.

Hold a candle to something
Meaning: Measure up to something
Example: It was apparent that his technical knowledge couldn't *hold a candle to* hers when he was not able to answer the client's questions during the conference call.

Hold one's fire
Meaning: To refrain from criticism or aggression
Example: If you don't *hold your fire*, you might be sorry later.

Hold one's horses
Meaning: To be patient and restrain from action
Example: It is better to *hold your horses* and wait to assess the situation before choosing the best action plan.

Hold one's tongue
Meaning: To refrain from speaking, even though one is tempted
Example: Though Jessie was tempted to answer when Bob asked her opinion of her boss, she decided to *hold her tongue* instead.

Hold the bag
Meaning: To be responsible for something, often even without involvement in it
Example: Craig was left *holding the bag* when his partner secretly left the country with their clients' investments.

Hot off the press
Meaning: Newly made public or released
Example: The news that the company is going public is *hot off the press*. It was just reported this morning.

In bed together
Meaning: Conspiring with someone
Example: Both political parties were **in bed together** during the corruption scandal.

In full swing
Meaning: When a task is at the highest level of activity
Example: The moment we decided to start the company, we moved right **into full swing** with our specific plans for how to become successful quickly.

In the bag
Meaning: Guaranteed; something that is assured
Example: He knew that the deal was **in the bag** because of his friendly relationship with the other company's CFO.

In the know
Meaning: Possessing special knowledge
Example: Because this project was performed confidentially, only a few people were **in the know.**

In the thick of something
Meaning: In the most intense part of something
Example: The publication team members were **in the thick of** an argument with the marketing team when the editors finally told everyone to calm down and take a break.

In the trenches
Meaning: In the most arduous part of something
Example: Often, in order to reach a top management job, you have start **in the trenches** of unpaid internships.

Iron out difficulties
Meaning: To work out or resolve differences
Example: It is imperative that you two **iron out your difficulties** with each other so that we can be a functional team.

Joined at the hip
Meaning: Very closely connected
Example: The regional manager and the assistant manager have been **joined at the hip** since they were roommates in college; they never disagree on any issue.

Jump-start someone (or something)
Meaning: To motivate or to spark production
Example: A good boss will give his employees incentive in order to **jump-start** their work.

Jump through hoops

Meaning: To go far beyond regular capacity in order to please someone or to complete some task

Example: My contract was incentive-laden, so near the end of the year I was ***jumping through hoops*** to get more deals completed.

Keep a lid on something

Meaning: Maintain confidentiality; not speak of something

Example: When the IRS investigated the company, they found that only the CFO knew about the company's tax fraud. He had ***kept a lid on*** his illegal activities for over ten years.

Keep all the balls in the air

Meaning: To maintain focus on all of one's responsibilities

Example: She was the best assistant I ever had. She always ***kept all the balls in the air*** and I rarely had to ask her to do anything twice.

Kick the habit

Meaning: To quit a regular activity that one feels is bad for their well being

Example: Many offices have now banned smoking breaks in order to increase production and to help smokers ***kick the habit*** of smoking throughout the day.

Kick the tires

Meaning: To check or test something before investing in or buying it

Example: I would advise you to ***kick the tires*** before you sign any contract with that manufacturer.

Origin: The actions of people purchasing cars.

Know which side one's bread is buttered on

Meaning: To be cognizant of whom one is receiving support from

Example: He really should give his boss a little more respect. Doesn't he ***know which side his bread is buttered on***?

Labor of love

Meaning: Work that is done for the joy it brings the person who is doing it

Example: While investment banking is exhausting work, it is a ***labor of love*** for some people, which makes the long hours manageable.

Land on one's feet

Meaning: To come through a difficult time with the ability to function normally

Example: James lost his job recently. He's really smart though, so I'm sure he'll ***land on his feet*** at another firm.

Lay an egg

Meaning: To do badly at some task

Example: The new employee was asked do easy work on Excel and he absolutely ***laid an egg***. He couldn't even do the simplest commands.

Left-handed compliment; back-handed compliment
Meaning: A comment that seems to be commending someone, but is actually an insult

Example: When my boss told me, "You did a good job for someone who has little experience," I was happy at first, but then I realized it was really just a ***left-handed compliment***.

Leg up (on someone)
Meaning: When one has a distinct advantage over someone else

Example: Since Jane had worked on Excel for years as a personal assistant, she had a ***leg up on*** me because the program was totally new to me.

Let off steam
Meaning: To do or say something that lets a person release tension they have been holding

Example: After work, Tom often goes to have a drink at the local bar. That's where he and his colleagues ***let off steam*** about how much they hate their jobs.

Let one's hair down
Meaning: To relax and enjoy oneself

Example: It took Jamie six months at the office to finally ***let her hair down*** and let her true personality show.

Like a house on fire
Meaning: With lots of enthusiasm and energy

Example: Once they found out their bonuses were performance-based, they started working ***like a house on fire***!

Likely story
Meaning: When someone uses an excuse that the listener does not believe is true

Example: Janine is always missing work. She called the office again today to say that she can't come in because her cat died. That's a ***likely story***. I don't think she even HAS a cat!

Lip service (to pay or give)
Meaning: To support someone/something with words, but the support is not sincere

Example: My boss pays ***lip service*** to my ideas, but he never lets me try any of them in our office.

Long shot
Meaning: Something that has a low chance of being successful

Example: With a GPA in the low 3's and a GMAT score of 520, he's a ***long shot*** for getting into any business schools.

Loose cannon
Meaning: someone who has an often uncontrollable and unpredictable temper

Example: You shouldn't cross our manager. He's such a ***loose cannon*** that it's probably smart to just do whatever he tells you.

Loose lips sink ships

Meaning: People who reveal confidential information cause dangerous results.

Example: When our boss tells us to keep certain internal information confidential, we listen to him. *Loose lips sink ships* and other employees have lost their jobs because they didn't protect information.

Lord it over someone

Meaning: To act like you are better than other people

Example: Just because Tanya closed a big deal, she shouldn't *lord it over* her colleagues. After all, they helped to get her to where she is in the company.

Lose one's marbles

Meaning: To act strangely; become a little crazy

Example: After spending 36 straight hours at the office, the investment banker began to *lose his marbles.* He couldn't even sit up straight in his chair anymore.

Magic bullet

Meaning: A savior or unexpected cure

Example: The financial services firm hired an economic advisor last year and she turned out to be their *magic bullet.* The following year's balance sheet showed a huge profit.

Make a mountain out of a molehill

Meaning: When someone makes a big deal out of a small event

Example: John is always punctual, but the one time he was late, his boss *made a mountain out of a molehill* and got really angry with him. That kind of reaction was totally unnecessary.

Make a person tick

Meaning: The beliefs and feelings that make someone act the way they act

Example: Jane and I are an excellent team at work. We really know what *makes the other person tick.*

Meet one's match

Meaning: To face a person who is of equal quality to, oneself or maybe even better

Example: After being the top salesperson for seven months in a row, Bob *met his match* in the new salesman. The new guy sold 4 more cars than Bob this month.

Mellow out

Meaning: To relax; take a break from any concerns

Example: When I saw that Michelle was becoming stressed about her assignment, I told her to go take a break and *mellow out.*

Muddy the waters

Meaning: To make something unclear or confusing

Example: The new analyst really needs to improve. His reports go off on tangents and his excessive wording and unrelated examples **muddy the waters** and make the reports unhelpful.

Necessary evil

Meaning: Something that is not liked, but is necessary

Example: I hate flying, but because much of our business is located out of the country, going on planes is a **necessary evil** for me.

Nip something in the bud

Meaning: To stop a potentially harmful situation just as it's beginning to develop

Example: Over the past week we've caught three people trying to shoplift from the store. We should **nip this trend in the bud** by installing security devices immediately.

Nodding acquaintance

Meaning: Refers to a person who is known to one on a superficial basis (so that, in passing, only a nod is required to acknowledge that person)

Example: I've met Jennifer a couple times in the office, but I still consider her a **nodding acquaintance** since we've never really spoken.

Nothing to be sneezed at

Meaning: Something that should not be dismissed easily – one should actually give it serious attention

Example: The manager's warning to show up to meetings on time is **nothing to be sneezed at**. He's fired employees for lesser reasons.

Note of concern

Meaning: A subtle hint of worry

Example: I sense a **note of concern** in your voice when you speak about the merger between your company and that bigger one.

Nurse a grudge

Meaning: To consciously maintain resentment against another person

Example: I know that Tom offended you, but **nursing a grudge** against him is not going to help anything.

1.3   O - Z

On the back burner

Meaning: To lessen the priority of something

Example: When we heard about our competitor's new strategy, we put everything else we were doing **on the back burner** until we figured out how to counter their actions.

On the fly
Meaning: When something is completed quickly, and without preparation
Example: I'm surprised that my boss was so happy with my report. I did it **on the fly**, and was worried about his reaction.

One for the books
Meaning: A classic event; something that will be remembered
Example: The real estate deal we pulled off was **one for the books**. I can't believe we were able to get a buyer for triple the amount we paid for the property.

Pet peeve
Meaning: An action or activity that consistently bothers one
Example: The employees were supposed to stay at the office until 5:00 PM, but often they would leave at 4:50 or 4:55. This was the boss's biggest **pet peeve** and he warned them to stay until 5 repeatedly.

Pick someone's brains
Meaning: To try to get information from a person who is knowledgeable about the subject
Example: Before I left to go to Barcelona for a business meeting, I **picked Javier's brains** about where the best restaurants were in the city. He's originally from Barcelona and knows a lot about it.

Play one's cards right
Meaning: To make strategic decisions that ultimately lead to the desired result
Example: If you **play your cards right** and impress the manager with your enthusiasm and dedication, you can get a promotion within the first six months.

Play the devil's advocate
Meaning: To take a different point of view deliberately in order to explore the other side of the issue
Example: It's nice to bounce my ideas off of my business partner. She will often **play the devil's advocate** so we can see all angles of the argument before we make a final decision.

Pull one's punches
Meaning: To deliberately keep one's opinions or influence to oneself, often to prove a point
Example: During our weekly office meetings, the boss often **pulls his punches** to evaluate whether or not we can arrive at the same conclusion without his guidance.

Pull out all the stops
Meaning: To utilize all resources to accomplish an objective
Example: We needed to sell more product than our closest competitor this month in order to win a huge new account, so we **pulled out all the stops** and worked throughout the night.

Pull something off

Meaning: To complete a task that may have been difficult

Example: I can't believe he **pulled off** rewriting that whole contract overnight! It was accidentally shredded yesterday and he must have stayed up all night writing it again.

Pull the plug on something

Meaning: To stop doing or producing something

Example: When we reported a loss for the fiscal year, the company had to **pull the plug on** a couple divisions that just weren't producing enough income.

Pull the rug out from under someone

Meaning: To very suddenly change a situation, therefore surprising other people

Example: Our division was having a record sales year, but then suddenly corporate just **pulled the rug out from under** us and told us our division was going to close.

Push one's buttons

Meaning: To upset a person by using approaches one knows will upset that person

Example: She knows that the manager can't handle when people whine, so when she really wants to **push his buttons**, she immediately starts to whine to him.

Push the envelope

Meaning: To test the limits

Example: That company really **pushes the envelope.** with their advertisements. I'm surprised the television networks will show those kinds of images.

Put on your thinking cap

Meaning: To concentrate deeply on something in order to find a solution

Example: When an important decision needs to be made, the boss always tells everybody to stop all other activity and **put on their thinking caps.**

Put one's foot in one's mouth

Meaning: To say/do something that you should not have (and is usually embarrassing to someone else)

Example: When Pam told her manager the real reason Karen was out of the office, she knew that she had put her **foot in her mouth**. Karen's now going to be reprimanded.

Put one's two cents in

Meaning: To offer one's opinion

Example: I'm no expert, but if you want me to **put my two cents in**, I would tell you to advertise over the internet.

Put something on the map

Meaning: To bring attention to something

Example: The founder of this company single-handedly **put it on the map** with his brilliant advertising.

Raise eyebrows

Meaning: Something that causes surprise and draws people's attention (sometimes with disapproval)

Example: When the CEO announced that he would be leaving the company, it **raised the eyebrows** of everybody who heard.

Raw deal

Meaning: An unfair outcome

Example: Jane thought she got a **raw deal** when John was promoted but she was not. She has worked at the company much longer than him.

Read someone like a book

Meaning: To understand someone very well

Example: Our boss can **read Jim like a book**. Before he even asked for the day off, she had already found someone to take over his responsibilities since she knew he'd be asking for the vacation.

Red herring

Meaning: A made-up circumstance that will divert people's attention away from the real issues

Example: Our boss said he fired Diane because she was not getting her work done. But we all knew that was a **red herring** and the real reason she got fired was because she embarrassed him.

Ring a bell

Meaning: When one hears/sees something that seems familiar to them

Example: When my secretary told me William Franklin was on the telephone, I knew the name **rang a bell**, but I couldn't remember exactly who he was.

Rock the boat

Meaning: To disrupt the current order of things

Example: When the new employee suggested some changes for our office, she was advised not to **rock the boat**.

Rub someone the wrong way

Meaning: To make a bad impression on somebody

Example: Even though my coworkers liked the new job candidate, something about her **rubbed me the wrong way**. I didn't trust her for some reason.

Ruffle someone's feathers

Meaning: When someone's actions upset another person

Example: I can't believe Tom would just not show up to work without telling his manager. That really **ruffled the manager's feathers**.

Run-in

Meaning: A confrontation or encounter (usually with bad consequences)

Example: We had a little **run-in** with the IRS. Apparently we forgot to file all of our tax returns for the previous fiscal year.

Run something past someone

Meaning: When one checks with another person before proceeding with something

Example: Before I go ahead and enter this data, I wanted to **run it past you** and make sure this is exactly what you wanted me to do.

Scrape the bottom of the barrel

Meaning: To be left with the least desirable choice

Example: I can't believe we're hiring an analyst with such little experience. We must really be **scraping the bottom of the barrel** if this candidate is the best we can find.

Shape up or ship out

Meaning: To be ordered to change one's attitude/behavior or otherwise be dismissed

Example: When sales were at an all-time low, the manager told all the salespeople to **shape up or ship out**. The following month ended with record high sales numbers.

Shoot from the hip

Meaning: To be forthright and not censor one's words

Example: Much of the reason for the CEO's success is that he **shoots from the hip.** This personality trait is admirable to many people.

Shoot oneself in the foot

Meaning: To say or do something that then causes problems for oneself

Example: He almost convinced the investor to buy his company, but he **shot himself in the foot** when he admitted the market was on its way down. The investor quickly withdrew his offer.

Shoot the breeze

Meaning: To casually converse with someone

Example: Even though we do lots of business with Bob's company, whenever he and I get together we rarely talk business. Instead, we normally just **shoot the breeze.**

Short end of the stick

Meaning: When one gets the least-desirable result in a situation

Example: John got the **short end of the stick** when his office was the only one that did not get remodeled over the holidays.

Short fuse

Meaning: The predisposition for getting upset easily

Example: I would advise you not to cross your new manager. He's got a **short fuse,** and even the smallest mistake can result in him becoming very angry.

Shot in the arm
Meaning: Something that motivates one to act
Example: When our boss told us that we would start receiving a commission on our sales, it was a big *shot in the arm* for everybody. Sales really skyrocketed.

Sit tight
Meaning: To wait patiently until further notice
Example: Once we sent our sales figures to our corporate office, all we could do was *sit tight* and wait to see if we met their expectations or not.

Sitting pretty
Meaning: To be in a good situation
Example: The owner's son was *sitting pretty*. Once he graduated from college, we all knew he was going to be able to take over the company without having to work his way up.

Slip of the tongue
Meaning: Something said by accident, not meant to be said
Example: It was a pretty serious *slip of the tongue* for our CEO to announce our quarterly numbers prematurely. As a result, many would-be investors decided to put their money elsewhere.

Smoke screen
Meaning: An action or statement that is used to hide something else
Example: The CEO's philanthropic donations were just a *smoke screen* that covered up millions of dollars that she embezzled from the company.

Smoking gun
Meaning: Something that acts as proof of immoral or illegal activity
Example: The *smoking gun* that allowed authorities to confirm that the CEO was embezzling money was her penchant for buying cars and homes that she could have never afforded on her salary alone.

Speak volumes
Meaning: Something that reveals lots of information about something else
Example: The billionaire's tendency to leave large tips and to donate huge amounts of money to charity *speaks volumes* about his character.

Split hairs
Meaning: To argue about small, silly things
Example: When her boss told her that she did a terrible job because her report was printed in size 11 font instead of size 11.5, we all thought he was *splitting hairs* for no good reason.

Stick to one's guns
Meaning: To continue focusing on that which one is committed to or that which one is good at
Example: I really admire our new chairman. He made his case for getting his position based on lower costs and higher output and **stuck to his guns** throughout, eventually getting the job.

Sticking point
Meaning: An issue that inhibits the forward progress of a negotiation
Example: The player's union could not agree with the basketball league about a new contract. The **sticking point** was that the league did not want to insure the players' bodies against injury.

Take a page from someone's book
Meaning: To imitate someone else's successful strategy or habit
Example: James is a conscientious and efficient worker. You should **take a page from his book** if you want to be competitive in this industry.

Take something by storm
Meaning: To have an immediate and very strong impact upon something
Example: When our new chewing gum entered the marketplace, we **took the market by storm**, selling the gum faster than we could produce it.

Tall order
Meaning: An expectation that is hard to meet
Example: Getting the report done by the end of the week was a **tall order**, but I did it by staying in the office all night.

The ball is in one's court

Meaning: To say that one is in control of the situation; the decision is theirs

Example: After the potential buyers made a counter offer, the **ball was once again in the seller's court**.

Related Expressions:

Drop the ball

Meaning: Fail to do the designated task up to standard

Example: Weren't you supposed to call to confirm that delivery? You really **dropped the ball** on that one, and now we won't have the shipment until after the weekend.

Carry the ball

Meaning: To take on responsibility for completing a task

Example: For each team sales project, a different person is chosen to **carry the ball**.

The right hand doesn't know what the left hand is doing

Meaning: When one one part of a group is unaware of the other's actions

Example: You would think that our CEO and COO would consult each other before making big decisions for the company. Apparently, however, the **right hand doesn't know what the left hand is doing**. The COO had no idea that the CEO had ordered us to shut down the other branch.

There's the rub

Meaning: Used to show the reason why something is difficult

Example: My boss wants our company to sell more product than our competitor does, and he expects me to make this happen. However, they have double the salespeople that we do and **there's the rub**.

Throw one's weight around

Meaning: To use authority to get what one wants

Example: Our CEO used to work for the government, so when we are trying to get new building permits, he often **throws his weight around** to make sure we get what we need quickly.

Throw the book at someone

Meaning: To penalize someone in the strongest way possible

Example: Because our CEO embezzled so much money from our firm under the disguise of giving to charity, everyone at our firm wanted the courts to **throw the book at** him.

Too many irons in the fire

Meaning: Engaged in too many activities

Example: If you have **too many irons in the fire**, you will not be able to concentrate on any single goal. As a result, you will be less productive than if you choose to focus on just one project.

Twist one's arm

Meaning: To pressure someone into doing something

Example: I really didn't want to go to the conference in San Diego, but my boss ***twisted my arm***, so I finally said I would go.

Chapter 2

Useful Euphemisms

2.1   Adjectives

Affordable
Meaning: Financially feasible; inexpensive; cheap
Example: I found an amazing restaurant with the most *affordable* food and cock-
tails for dinner!

Related expressions:

Budget
Meaning: Within a financial limit.
Example: We stayed at a **budget** hotel, but it was very nice and clean.

Budget constraints (noun)
Meaning: Financial limits
Example: The company was forced to cut down on costs due to **budget constraints**.

Careful with one's money (phrase)
Meaning: Financial caution.
Example: Our boss is very **careful with his money**.

Close with one's money (phrase)
Meaning: Stingy; not generous with money
Example: Don't ask Chuck for a contribution to the bonus pool for all the assistants! He is so **close with his money** that it is not possible for him to chip in even just a few bucks.

Finances (noun)
Meaning: Referring to money or assets
Example: I want to buy a new car, but I don't have the **finances**.
Synonyms: capital, dough, moolah, the means

Thrifty
Meaning: Frugal
Example: Our firm needs another employee because we're growing so rapidly, but my partner is so **thrifty** that he'd rather spend twenty hours a day in the office instead of hiring extra help.

Appropriate
Meaning: Acceptable; correct; polite
Example: Certain jokes are not **appropriate** in an office setting.

Awkward
Meaning: Difficult or humiliating
Example: It would be **awkward** if my boss finds out that I am doing some marketing research for one of our competitors.

Challenged
Meaning: Having difficulty completing a task
Example: My colleague is a great writer, but a bit **challenged** when it comes to dealing with numbers. That, however, is where I can be helpful.

Related Expressions:

Impaired
Meaning: Incapable of mentally or physically doing something
Example: Learning-impaired students often get extended time to do their tests.

Chubby
Meaning: Overweight, heavy
Example: He's a little on the **chubby** side, but he is still very attractive.

Creative
Meaning: Not truthful
Example: Mandy had a very **creative** way of balancing the books for her company.

Related Expressions:

Baloney (noun)
Meaning: Ridiculous or false
Example: Give me the true story, not some **baloney**!

Disingenuous
Meaning: Withholding information; not truthful
Example: His reason for not giving us a raise was **disingenuous,** and we all knew it.

Evasion (noun)
Meaning: A deceitful statement
Example: I am fed up with all the **evasions** that our management has told us. Is there a merger or not?

Imaginative
Meaning: Not entirely honest
Example: He was very **imaginative** when he decided to write off some expenses on his tax report.

Inflated
Meaning: Overstated; not true
Example: The company's quarterly report **inflated** what their actual earnings were because they needed to make their stockholders happy.

On the up and up (phrase)
Meaning: Fair; honest; legitimate (usually used in the negative)
Example: I wouldn't deal with that broker. Her reputation is that she's not **on the up and up.**

Selective
Meaning: Dishonest
Example: He was quite *selective* in telling his boss the reasons the tasks didn't get completed.

White lie (noun)
Meaning: A lie with good intention behind it
Example: When she showed up late to work, I had already told our boss a *white lie* for her about how her dog had been sick.

Inclusive
Meaning: Without prejudice or bias
Example: We should use *inclusive* language in our report so that it addresses the needs of all parties.

Less fortunate
Meaning: Underprivileged; without money
Example: Many companies devote lots of money and time to the *less fortunate* during the holiday season.

Mellow
Meaning: Intoxicated
Example: After all the cocktails he drank at the office party, he appeared really *mellow*.

2.2   Nouns & Phrasal Nouns

Adjustment
Meaning: A reduction
Example: The unexpected *adjustment* in my salary was announced by my boss this afternoon. I have to cut down on my expenses now that I'm going to have a smaller paycheck.

Administrative assistant
Meaning: A secretarial position
Example: Please schedule the appointment with my *administrative assistant.*

Amenities
Meaning: Typically referring to restroom facilities
Example: No wonder the hotel is so affordable! It only offers shared *amenities.*

Anomaly
Meaning: Something wrong; an unsatisfactory and unexpected inconsistency
Example: He is usually very accurate. His last research article must be an *anomaly!* After some basic auditing of the financial statements, we have found some *anomalies* in a few assets accounts. We will explore a bit further to find out the source.

Assistance
Meaning: Financial aid, typically from the government
Example: The government should offer those veterans more generous *assistance* for their past service to our country!

Bad language
Meaning: Cursing; vulgar words
Example: *Bad language* is often used on the trading floor in a large bank.

Related Expressions:

Strong language
Meaning: Curses; swear words
Example: We know our boss is serious when he starts to use *strong language*.

Belief system
Meaning: A person's spiritual ideologies
Example: Spirituality does not have to be based on a common *belief system* such as Catholicism or Christianity.

Capacity
Meaning: A job
Example: Have you worked in a similar *capacity* to the position we are looking for?

Costume jewelry
Meaning: Jewelry that is not genuine
Example: You can hardly tell that necklace is *costume jewelry.*

Counsel
Meaning: An attorney or lawyer
Example: "Will the *counsel* please step to the bench?" asked the judge impatiently.

Courtesy
Meaning: Offered or included for free
Example: Most high-class hotels offer a *courtesy* continental breakfast.

Displaced person
Meaning: A refugee
Example: After the war, the government had a meeting to decide on how to deal with the large number of *displaced persons.*

Event

Meaning: An unfortunate incident
Example: What an *event* today! My company just cut 20 jobs.
Synonym: Episode, Incident

Related Expressions:

Incident
Meaning: A horrible mishap
Example: The *incident* where the company faulted on their lease left them in breach of contract.

Golden handshake
Meaning: Compensation given to an employee that has been let go from his job (the amount is typically higher than regular severance pay)
Example: The only thing that stopped her from filing a law suit against her former employer was the *golden handshake* he offered her.

Related Expressions:

Golden parachute
Meaning: The compensation contractually promised to an employee (typically in a higher level position) if he is fired
Example: His *golden parachute* is so generous that he sometimes wished he would be fired.

Structured environment
Meaning: An organization with firm rules
Example: She left the firm because the *structured environment* there was too rigid for her to handle.

Visitation
Meaning: When people come together to pay tribute to someone who has recently died and to view the dead body
Example: Please come to the *visitation* on Thursday with me so we can cheer up the family. I believe the funeral will be Friday morning.

2.3   Verbs & Phrasal Verbs

Cover up
Meaning: Conceal or hide the truth
Example: The analyst made a serious mistake in the presentation book. He tried to *cover up*, but was still found out by his team members.

Doctor
Meaning: Alter something with bad intentions
Example: Don't *doctor* the books! Your auditor will figure it out quickly.

Related Expressions:

Finesse (verb)
Meaning: To achieve an objective through less than honest means
Example: Even though he is not very capable, he somehow *finessed* his way to top management.

Stretch the truth (phrase)
Meaning: To be dishonest
Example: When he bragged to his friends about his salary, he was *stretching the truth*. His actual income was much less than what he said.

Step down
Meaning: To leave a job (usually from a prominent position)
Example: What do we have to do to get the new CEO to *step down*?

2.4   Adverbs

Less than
Meaning: Not meeting expectations
Example: My boss told me she has been *less than* thrilled with my performance lately.

2.5   Phrases & Sentences

Bend the rules
Meaning: Compromising set standards; to be flexible
Example: The Company's vacation policy may seem strict, but they've been known to *bend the rules* occasionally.

Bring someone to justice
Meaning: Punish a person who is guilty of a crime
Example: "You have been *brought to justice*", the judge told the young delinquent.

Close its doors
Meaning: Go out of business
Example: My favorite coffee shop has *closed its doors!*

I hear you
Meaning: I heard what you said but I have a different opinion.
Example: *I hear you*, but I think that if we bought that stock we'd be taking a huge risk for little gain.

Related Expressions:

Take something under advisement

Meaning: To consider something (often connotes that it will be ignored; used for more formal occasions)

Example: I came up with some great ideas for the new ad campaign. My boss said she'd **take my ideas under advisement**. I guess she didn't like them as much as I did.

I'll let you go

Meaning: I have to get off the phone with you now.

Example: My meeting is about to start, so I'm going to **let you go**.

Not quite right

Meaning: Not mentally stable or capable

Example: Sometimes I don't understand how the guy in the next cubicle got hired. He's **not quite right** in the head.

Synonyms: *A few bricks short of a load, a few cards short of a full deck, a few enchiladas short of a combination plate, have bats in the belfry, loony, loopy, mental, nuts, nutty, off one's rocker, round the bend.*

Chapter 3

Workplace Slang & Idioms

3.1 General Business Descriptions

Fly-by-night operation
Function: Noun
Meaning: An untrustworthy business that tries to make a quick and easy profit
Example: That online retailer runs a *fly-by-night operation,* so be careful when ordering anything from them.

Gold mine
Function: Noun
Meaning: A very successful business
Example: The small business that I've started from my garage has really turned into a *gold mine*!
Synonym: *cash cow; big seller; smash hit (typically used for products, songs or movies only)*

Line of business
Function: Noun
Meaning: The kind of work or occupation that someone does.
Example: What *line of business* is she in?

Make a buck
Function: Verb
Meaning: To make money
Example: When I first moved to NYC, I couldn't *make a buck*, but since I started my online blog, I have been invited to all types of events as a speaker.
Synonym: *make an honest buck; make big bucks (to make a lot of money)*

Racket
Function: Noun
Meaning: An illegal business that deceives people
Example: Every day Bruno receives mailing advertising for 10× returns on an immediate investment of $10,000 in the recommended stocks, but that just sounds like a *racket* and he ignores the offer.

Seat-of-the-pants operation

Function: Noun
Meaning: A business driven by instinct and speculation
Example: Even though that one-man shop is a **seat-of-the-pants operation**, it has proven to be very successful.

Set up shop

Function: Verb
Meaning: To start a business
Example: My family and I are going to **set up shop** next week. Please come to the grand opening of our restaurant!

Small-time

Function: Adjective
Meaning: Little, trivial; when applied to a business, one which does not make significant money
Example: Daniel started with a **small-time** business, but now that business has grown into a multi-million dollar industry.
Antonym: big-time business

3.2   Corporate Hierarchy

3.2.1   Job descriptions by position type

Desk jockey

Function: Noun
Meaning: Someone who works at a desk all day
Example: Susan is tired of being a **desk jockey** . She's going to make a big career change and looks forward to her new job as a swimming coach.

Flunky

Function: Noun
Meaning: A person who does unskilled tasks for a boss
Example: Right now I'm only one of Mr. Smith's **flunkies**, but one day I plan to own my own company.

Gofer

Function: Noun
Meaning: Someone who runs errands for others
Example: When I started in the company, I was just a **gofer,** but now look at me!

Grease monkey

Function: Noun
Meaning: A mechanic
Example: Even though I'm a **grease monkey,** I make as much money as some office professionals!

Hired gun
Function: Noun
Meaning: A person hired by a business to take care of complex legal or business problems
Example: Hillary Smith is the veteran corporate lawyer I told you about; she is our new **hired gun**.

Hired hand
Function: Noun
Meaning: An employee who is hired to be an "extra hand" for the boss.
Example: Tom is our new **hired hand**. He'll be helping me package orders every morning.

Paper-pusher
Function: Noun
Meaning: A clerical desk worker whose tasks include boring administrative tasks that require large amounts of paper work
Example: For the past year, I've been a **paper-pusher** in this law firm.

Techie
Function: Noun
Meaning: A technician
Example: Debbie is one of the best **techies** I've ever met. She knows everything about computers.

3.2.2   Job descriptions by influence level

Big wig
Function: Noun
Meaning: Executive; an important decision-maker; someone in charge
Example: Tom used to work for me, but since his promotion, he has become a **big wig** in the company now.
Synonym: *the top brass/the big brass/the brass; big shot; big cheese; chief; higher ups (typically in plural); top dog; big enchilada; big wheel*

Working stiff
Function: Noun
Meaning: An employee who does not hold great responsibilities in his/her place of work
Example: Ruth is okay with being a **working stiff**, but her husband wants her to try and get a better corporate position.

Yuppie

Function: Noun

Meaning: An abbreviation for "young urban professional"; someone who has a well paid professional job and a materialistic lifestyle

Example: He is such a *yuppie,* working hard but having a weekend getaway at least once every month!

3.2.3 Job descriptions by work style

Dead wood

Function: Noun

Meaning: An employee who does not do any work

Example: Tina is nothing but *dead wood*. I don't understand why she hasn't been fired yet!

Hunt-and-peck typist

Function: Noun

Meaning: A person who types by looking at each key because he has not memorized the keyboard

Example: Artie is a *hunt-and peck typist* and that is why it takes him so long to finish a task.

Slave driver

Function: Noun

Meaning: An employer who demands constant work from his employees

Example: Our new boss demands an incredible amount of work from us all of the time. She's definitely a *slave driver*.

Workhorse

Function: Noun

Meaning: A person who works vigorously

Example: Hannah is a *workhorse*; she gets all her projects done on time.

3.3 Performance Review

3.3.1 Work style

Be on one's toes

Function: Verb

Meaning: To be alert and prepared

Example: *Be on your toes* today because all of the executives are going to be here for a meeting.

Bust one's buns
Function: Verb
Meaning: To work extremely hard in order to accomplish a task
Example: I am upset because even though I **busted my buns** all week to get this project finished, I was still not given the appreciation I deserved for my work.
Synonym: bust one's ass (crude yet very popular); break one's neck

Busy as a beaver (to be as); to be a busy [little] bee
Function: Verb
Meaning: To be very busy
Example: I wasn't able to sit down for even a second yesterday because I was as **busy as a beaver** all day.

Do something by the book
Function: Verb
Meaning: To follow the rules precisely
Example: My new boss **does everything by the book**. She won't even let me take five extra minutes for lunch.

Jump through hoops
Function: Verb
Meaning: To go through pointless tasks to fulfill a person's or a bureaucracy's expectations
Example: I've been **jumping through hoops** to try and get my visa extended, but so far I haven't been successful.

On the clock
Function: Noun
Meaning: The time period during which you are being paid to do work (most applicable to attorneys, consultants, etc.)
Example: I'll give you a call during my lunch break because I'm not allowed to talk on the phone while I'm **on the clock**.

Plug away at something
Function: Verb
Meaning: To work determinedly and steadily on something
Example: I've been **plugging away at** this book for almost three years. I should be done in just a few more days!

Pull one's weight
Function: Verb
Meaning: To do his/her own share of work
Example: Pat is going to get fired if he doesn't start to **pull his weight** around here.

Put one's nose to the grindstone
Function: Verb
Meaning: To concentrate and work diligently on something
Example: You must **put your nose to the grindstone** because the project must be completed within a week.

Wear several [different] hats
Function: Verb
Meaning: To have many [different] duties or responsibilities
Example: Erica **wears many different hats**; she's a medical doctor, volunteer, and a mother.

Work like a dog
Function: Verb
Meaning: To work very hard
Example: Annette **worked like a dog** in order to get the project done by the deadline.

Work one's fingers to the bone
Function: Verb
Meaning: To work very hard
Example: I **work my fingers to the bone** every day, and yet I still don't think that Mr. Rogers appreciates the work that I do for him.

3.3.2   Job review related

Be/get called on the carpet
Function: Verb
Meaning: To get reprimanded (by a boss, parents, etc); to be blamed; to be scolded
Example: I was **called on the carpet** for the way I didn't follow company rules.
Synonym: *get chewed out*

Buck for a raise
Function: Verb
Meaning: To be very determined about getting a salary raise
Example: Johnson has been working harder than anyone else these past couple of months because he is **bucking for a raise.**

Bumped up
Function: Verb
Meaning: 1. To get promoted in ranks; 2. To get a salary raise
Example: 1: I am so happy because after three years of hard work I finally got **bumped up** to vice president!
            2: My salary got **bumped up** this morning and now I'm being paid twice as much as before.

Cut out to be something
Function: Adjective
Meaning: To be suited to doing something
Example: David isn't **cut out to be** an accountant; he isn't detail-oriented nor does he like numbers.

Head and shoulders above the competition
Function: Adjective
Meaning: To be more qualified than one's competitors
Example: Our software is **head and shoulders above** all the other software on the market. No one is able to compete with our superior technology!

Know the ropes
Function: Verb
Meaning: To know the procedures in a company
Example: I don't **know the ropes** because I've only been working here for a week.
Related: Show someone the ropes; learn the ropes

Talk a good game
Function: Verb
Meaning: To speak with self-confidence and expertise about something, but not actually be good at it
Example: Erik **talks a good game** but don't expect anything more than talk.

Up to par
Function: Adjective
Meaning: To satisfy acceptable standards
Example: My boss called me into his office and told me that my work was not **up to par** lately, and if I do not improve, then I will be fired.

3.4   Office Use

Don't make waves
Function: Sentence
Meaning: Don't create any problems.
Example: One piece of advice that I was given at my first job was that I **shouldn't make any waves** and that way I could keep my job.
Related: Don't stir it up! Don't rock the boat!

Go to bat for someone
Function: Verb
Meaning: To help someone by talking to someone else in support of them
Example: I'm going to **go to bat for** you tomorrow and ask the boss to give you a raise. Wish me luck!

Grunt work

Function: Noun
Meaning: Unskilled, physical labor that causes one to grunt
Example: I've been doing this **grunt work** all day: moving my boss's furniture from his old office to his new bigger office down the hall.

It's a dog eat dog world

Function: Sentence
Meaning: Describing a world in which only the strongest are able to survive
Example: You must be aggressive in business because **it's a dog eat dog world** out there.

It's a jungle out there

Function: Sentence
Meaning: Describing a very competitive business world
Example: **It's a jungle out there,** and that's why it's very hard for a small new company to become successful.
Related: The law of the jungle

Kiss up to someone

Function: Verb
Meaning: To compliment someone excessively in the hope of obtaining something like a promotion, a raise, a favor, etc.
Example: Have you noticed how Arlene has been **kissing up to** the boss lately? I really think that she wants a raise.
Related: Curry favor with (British use)

Odd jobs

Function: Noun
Meaning: Unspecialized and unrelated jobs
Example: When you have the time, I would like you to do some **odd jobs** around the house for me.

Pull some strings

Function: Verb
Meaning: To get something done by using one's influence
Example: Even though you aren't our ideal candidate, I was able to **pull some strings** with the boss and I got you an interview.

Rat race

Function: Noun
Meaning: The competitive and cutthroat business world
Example: Katherine got tired of the **rat race**, so now she lives in the country and raises chickens.

Scuttlebutt

Function: Noun
Meaning: The gossip that is related to the office
Example: What's the **scuttlebutt** about the CEO and the new employee?

The early bird gets the worm

Function:	Proverb
Meaning:	The person who wakes up the earliest (or who starts a project first) gets the best chance for success
Example:	Remember that in the business world, ***the early bird gets the worm***!

Water cooler gossip

Function:	Noun
Meaning:	Gossip exchanged between coworkers at the office water cooler
Example:	Even though it's only ***water cooler gossip***, I really do believe that there is something going on between Monica and William.

3.5 Work Flow & Project Management

3.5.1 Work flow

Back to the salt mines; back to the grind

Function:	Verb
Meaning:	A humorous way of saying "get back to work" (returning to undesirable tasks)
Example:	I've got to get ***back to the salt mines***; I can't believe my lunch hour is already over.

Call in sick

Function:	Phrase
Meaning:	To call one's place of work and say you will not come work because of an illness
Example:	I'm going to ***call in sick*** because I have an upset stomach this morning.

Call it a day; call it a night

Function:	Phrase
Meaning:	To stop working for the day
Example:	I've been here since six this morning so I think I'm going to ***call it a day.***

Call it quits

Function:	Phrase
Meaning:	To quit for the day or to quit permanently, depending on the context
Example:	I need to ***call it quits*** earlier than usual today because I have to pick my son up from school.

Knock off early

Function:	Verb
Meaning:	To leave work early
Example:	I have to ***knock off early*** today because I'm going out out for dinner with my husband.
Synonym:	***pack it in; pack up***

Make it in

Function: Verb

Meaning: To get to the office or home

Example: Sarah had to *make it in* early this morning because she had an eight o'clock meeting.

Nine-to-five

Function: Noun

Meaning: A full-time job which is typically from 9:00 AM to 5:00 PM

Example: I'm very proud of Michael because after years of working odd jobs, he finally got his first *nine-to-five*.

On/at lunch (to be)

Function: Verb

Meaning: To be on one's lunch break

Example: Jerry has been *on lunch* for over two hours; he's going to make our boss angry.

On the job

Function: Phrase

Meaning: During working hours

Example: Annette was caught shopping online while she was *on the job*. She was yelled at by the boss because that's against company policy.

Slack off

Function: Verb

Meaning: To decrease one's productivity level

Example: Arthur started to *slack off* after knew the boss was planning to fire him.

Related: Slacker

Step out

Function: Verb

Meaning: To go away temporarily

Example: Sophia *stepped out* of the meeting for a few minutes to take care of an emergency.

Take lunch

Function: Verb

Meaning: To go on one's lunch break

Example: Shelly *took lunch* early today because she has to go to a dental appointment.

Work graveyard; work the graveyard shift

Function: Verb

Meaning: To work the late-night shift from midnight to 8:00 AM

Example: I like to *work the graveyard shift* because that way I can do errands earlier in the day.

Synonym: work [the] swing shift

3.5.2 Project management

Back to the drawing board (to go)

Function: Verb

Meaning: To start a task or project all over again

Example: I guess I have to go **back to the drawing board** because my boss rejected my proposal, even after weeks of preparation and research.

Blood, sweat and tears

Function: Noun

Meaning: Describes something that takes a lot of hard work, mental stress and disappointments in order to be accomplished

Example: After a lot of **blood, sweat and tears,** I finally finished the proposal for the new hotel complex.

Bring someone up to speed

Function: Verb

Meaning: To give someone the most up-to-date information

Example: Robin was out sick yesterday, so I decided I should **bring her up to speed** on what she missed.

Buckle down

Function: Verb

Meaning: To make an extra effort to work harder than before in order to accomplish something

Example: We must **buckle down** to get this project finished before the boss comes back.

Carve out a niche

Function: Verb

Meaning: To make a place for yourself through hard work

Example: Arnold has really **carved out** a niche for himself writing his blog.

Cover for someone

Function: Verb

Meaning: To take on another person's responsibilities temporarily

Example: Can you **cover for** Linda tomorrow because she needs to take her son to a dental appointment?

Elbow grease

Function: Noun

Meaning: Extra hard physical effort to get something accomplished

Example: You need to put some more **elbow grease** into cleaning your car or it will never get clean.

Fill in for someone
Function: Verb
Meaning: To substitute for another employee temporarily
Example: I'm going to *fill in for* Rose while she's visiting her family in Florida.

Get cracking
Function: Verb
Meaning: To start working quickly
Example: You'd better *get cracking* on that assignment if you plan to finish before you leave on vacation.
Synonym: *get the ball rolling; get the show on the road*
Related: Take a crack at
Meaning: Try something

Get down to brass tacks; get down to business
Function: Verb
Meaning: To focus on the most important issues
Example: Let's *get down to brass tacks* right now because we only have four days to finish this task.
Synonym: *Get down to the nitty gritty*

Going great guns
Function: Verb
Meaning: To be moving ahead extremely well
Example: We're already *going great guns* despite the fact that we've only been open for a couple of weeks.

In the loop (to be)
Function: Adverb
Meaning: To be informed
Example: I would appreciate it if you kept me *in the loop* even though I'll be on vacation for the next two weeks.
Synonym: *to be in the know*

Murphy's law
Function: Noun
Meaning: A comical truth that states that "anything that can go wrong will go wrong"
Example: I was totally prepared for the meeting today, but I forgot my briefcase at home, then the subway train got delayed for an hour, and then the elevator was broken so I had to climb up twelve flights of stairs. *Murphy's law*!
Synonym: *Sod's law (British use)*

Need it yesterday

Function: Phrase

Meaning: A common phrase in the business world which means that something must be finished immediately

Example: Please add these pages to the report and hurry! I **need it yesterday**!

Variations: *Need it five minutes ago; need it last week*

No-brainer

Function: Noun

Meaning: A decision that is obvious

Example: Because our customer list was so big, the decision to expand our business was a **no-brainer**.

On the fly

Function: Adjective

Meaning: Used to express an action done either without much planning, or done while in motion

Example: I never make a decision **on the fly**. I like to think about all possible results.

Out of the loop

Function: Verb

Meaning: Not being informed of what is happening

Example: Tell me what happened in the office while I was out; I feel completely **out of the loop**!

Paper trail

Function: Noun

Meaning: Documented evidence of a person's actions

Example: We caught Johnson in his attempt to default the company because the **paper trail** led to him.

Pull the plug on the project

Function: Verb

Meaning: To end a project suddenly

Example: The boss decided to **pull the plug on the project** due to lack of funding.

Pull up a document/file

Meaning: To retrieve a computer document or file and put on your screen

Example: When you have a moment, I need you to **pull up the document** we were working on yesterday and make some changes.

Put a rush on something

Function: Verb

Meaning: To speed up the process on something

Example: You must **put a rush on** this project because our jobs are depending on its completion.

Reinvent the wheel
Function: Verb
Meaning: To recreate an already existing idea
Example: Why are you trying to **reinvent the wheel**? Just do it the way everyone does it.
Related: Spin one's wheels
Meaning: Work hard without making meaningful progress.
Origin: The expression comes from the situation in which a car cannot move forward despite its wheels spinning frenetically. Imagine a car getting stuck in snow or a rut.

Run the show
Function: Verb
Meaning: To be in charge
Example: I'm going to start **running the show** now that the boss has decided to step down.

3.6   Meetings and Conference Calls

Copy someone on something
Function: Verb
Meaning: To send a copy of a letter, memo, or email to someone
Example: Please **copy me on the letter** you're faxing to the CEO of the company.

Jot something down
Function: Verb
Meaning: To write something down quickly
Example: I should **jot that name down** so that I don't forget it.

Put something on the table
Function: Verb
Meaning: To put it on the agenda
Example: We need to update our website more frequently. Let's **put that on the table** in our next meeting.

Table the discussion
Function: Verb
Meaning: Postpone
Example: We are out of time. Let's **table the discussion** till we have more facts.

Under the table
Function: Adverb
Meaning: secretly
Example: Let's do the deal **under the table**. Let's be sure we get rid of the paper trail!

3.7 Personal finance

Bring home the bacon
Function:	Verb
Meaning:	To make money
Example:	Michael **brings home the bacon,** and Sharon raises the kids.

Cut back
Function:	Verb
Meaning:	To spend less
Example:	After careful review of the budget, it is necessary that we **cut back** on useless expenses this year.

Pay hike (To give someone a pay hike; to get a pay hike)
Function:	Noun
Meaning:	An increase in salary
Example:	My boss just gave me a **pay hike** and told me I'm doing a great job!

Perks
Function:	Noun
Meaning:	Special advantages one gets from his job (such as free medical coverage, car, gas, car insurance, etc.; also used for informal advantages
Example:	I'm getting some great **perks** with my new job - three weeks of vacation, and dental and medical benefits.
Synonym:	*extras; fringe benefits*

3.8 Hiring, Firing and Downsizing

Be between jobs
Function:	Adverb
Meaning:	A more positive and less offensive way of saying "to be unemployed"
Example:	I've been **between jobs** for a month, but I know that I'll find another one soon.

Can someone; get canned
Function:	Verb
Meaning:	To fire someone from a position (to can); to be the person who is fired (get canned)
Example:	Rob is going to **get canned** if he continues to come in late.
Synonym:	*give someone the axe; give someone the boot; boot someone out; get the boot; get the axe; sack someone; give someone the sack; give someone the heave-ho; get the heave-ho; give someone his walking papers; get one's walking papers; let someone go; be let go*

Cushy job
Function: Noun
Meaning: An extremely easy job
Example: Heather just got a **cushy job** as a fashion designer's assistant. She gets to fly all over the world with him, go to wonderful parties and do very little actual work.
Antonym: **grunt work**

Cutbacks
Function: Noun
Meaning: Reductions in the amount a business spends and/or the number of staff
Example: We need to make some **cutbacks** this year because the company lost money last year.

Downsize
Function: Verb
Meaning: To reduce the size of a company (such as personnel, budgets and physical space)
Example: The company will be **downsizing** this year which means that many employees will lose their jobs.

Get one's foot in the door
Function: Verb
Meaning: To begin working for a company in a low position, but with the hope of rising
Example: I just need to **get my foot in the door** and then I'll show the company how much they need me.

Hatchet man
Function: Noun
Meaning: The person given the task of laying off employees
Example: Because I'm the floor manager, I'm the **hatchet man** who fires the bad employees.

Have good contacts
Function: Verb
Meaning: To know people who can help one get ahead
Example: Because of my mother's **good contacts**, I got a job in the company I wanted.

Headhunter
Function: Noun
Meaning: A job recruiter who helps companies find candidates to fill executive positions
Example: Randy just received a call from a **headhunter** telling him that there is a major investment banking company that wants to meet him.

Hold down a job

Function: Verb

Meaning: To keep a job

Example: I'm very proud of Cynthia because she is able to take care of her family while **holding down two jobs**.

Knock on doors

Function: Verb

Meaning: To search for employment

Example: After **knocking on doors** for the past three weeks, I still haven't been able to find a job.

Land a job

Function: Verb

Meaning: To get a job

Example: I just **landed the job** of my dreams! I'm going to start working with the best fashion designer in New York City next week.

Lay off

Function: Verb

Meaning: To end someone's employment because the company doesn't need that person, or cannot afford to pay them

Example: The company lost a lot of money due to some bad investments. I think that they are going to start to **lay off** some employees.

Moonlight

Function: Verb

Meaning: To work a second job, typically at night

Example: Robert works in the mail room during the day and then he **moonlights** as a bartender at night.

One's job is on the line

Function: Expression

Meaning: To be in danger of losing one's job

Example: My job is **on the line** right now because my sales are so low.

Pound the pavement; go job hunting

Function: Verb

Meaning: To actively search for new employment

Example: I've been **pounding the pavement** for three weeks and I still can't find a job.

Synonym: **job hunt; knock on doors**

Trim the fat

Function: Verb

Meaning: To make reductions in personnel

Example: Because of the poor economy, we're going to have to **trim the fat** in our company if we want to survive.

Walk
Function: Verb
Meaning: To quit a job because of dissatisfaction with the employer
Example: We are going to *walk* if we don't get the seven percent raise that we want.

3.9   Negotiation and Conflict Resolutions

Back down
Function: Verb
Meaning: To retreat from a position during a negotiation
Example: The union looks like it is going to *back down* on the pension negotiations, so the strike will now be able to be settled.

Barter
Function: Verb
Meaning: To trade products or services without using money
Example: In ancient times before there was money, people would just *barter* for services needed.

Be at a standstill
Function: Verb
Meaning: To be in a situation where no further progress can be made
Example: We have been *at a standstill* for six weeks with the union now. The city is being hurt more than the union members.
Synonym: :come to a stop, come to a standstill, be at a deadlock, be at a stalemate, be at a standoff, hit a dead end

Blow a deal
Function: Verb
Meaning: To fail at a negotiation
Example: Anthony *blew the deal* when he asked the client for half of the money immediately.

Break down
Function: Verb
Meaning: Describing a negotiation that failed
Example: After hours of negotiating, the deal *broke down* because of issues we couldn't resolve.

Bring something to the table
Function: Verb
Meaning: To offer something during a negotiation; to have something to offer to a team or a company
Example: We should always try to learn new skills and acquire new knowledge on the job to ensure we have something valuable to *bring to the table.*

Call someone's bluff

Function: Verb
Meaning: To clearly show disbelief in someone's threat and to rebuff them
Example: Jim said if we didn't increase his salary, he'd go to a competitor. We **called his bluff** and told him our resources are tight. The next day, he said he would stay on for another year!

Cave; cave in

Function: Verb
Meaning: To comply by accepting someone's conditions
Example: Jim finally **caved to** the union after twenty hours of negotiations.
Synonym: *to buckle, to come around, cry/say uncle, give in/up, knuckle under, throw in the towel*

Come back with something

Function: Verb
Meaning: To come back with a different proposal
Example: We disagree with our landlord about the rent for the next lease term. I hope they will **come back with** a better offer next week! Otherwise I have to re-evaluate ours.

Come down

Function: Verb
Meaning: To reduce one's prices
Example: After three hours of negotiating, the manufacturer finally **came down to** a fifty percent discount.

Come Hell or high water

Function: Adverb
Meaning: Regardless of the difficulties
Example: I will honor my promise, **come hell or high water.**

Come in high

Function: Verb
Meaning: To ask for too much money for services rendered
Example: The car salesman is **coming in high**, and I think it would be best if he renegotiates this deal with us.

Dicker

Function: Verb
Meaning: To bargain; to negotiate for a lower price or a better deal (use with caution; a bit offensive)
Example: This is the first time in five years that our suppliers have increased prices. You might offend them if you try to **dicker** over the price tag.
Synonym: *haggle*

Do some fence-mending
Function: Verb
Meaning: To restore a relationship (as you would repair a broken fence between two neighbors)
Example: Joe and Ted have refused to speak to each other since their argument, but they're going to have to **do some fence-mending** because the boss wants them to work together on a project.

Drive a hard bargain
Function: Verb
Meaning: To be a very well trained and demanding negotiator
Example: I **drove a hard bargain** when I went to the car dealership and got a great price on my new car.

Fall through
Function: Verb
Meaning: Describing an unsuccessful negotiation or a deal that does not come to fruition
Example: The deal **fell through** after our disastrous client meeting. Our pitches could not match those of our competitors.

Get in bed with someone
Function: Verb
Meaning: To begin a close working relationship with someone
Example: We should be cautious with this client. I do not know much about him except that he had a bad credit history. We need to be sure we really want to **get in bed with** him.

Get the raw end of the deal
Function: Verb
Meaning: To get an undesirable result in a negotiation
Example: You lowered your selling price by 20 percent and you still absorbed shipping costs? It sounds to me like you **got the raw end of the deal!**
Synonym: *get the short end of the stick*

Give a little
Function: Verb
Meaning: To be able to compromise in a negotiation
Example: Sometimes you have to be willing to **give a little**. Even the best negotiators don't always get the exact deals they want.

Give and take
Function: Noun
Meaning: A compromise, an exchange
Example: After a lot of **give and take** from both sides, we all came to an agreement.

Give away the farm
Function: Verb
Meaning: To offer more than is necessary during a negotiation
Example: We don't want to divulge too much information early in the negotiation process. Don't let Charles negotiate for us. Last time he **gave away the farm!**

Go-between
Function: Noun
Meaning: A negotiator or mediator who acts as the link between parties
Example: Leighton is the **go-between** for the city and the union.
Synonym: *middle-man*

Go sour
Function: Verb
Meaning: Describing a negotiation that collapses
Example: The negotiations between the city and the union were looking good, but they suddenly **went sour** when the city refused the pension package designed by the union.
Synonyms: break down; fall apart; fall through

Hammer out a deal
Function: Verb
Meaning: To reach an agreement
Example: Due to two great negotiators working together, they were able to **hammer out a deal** in less than an hour.
Synonyms: to clinch a deal, to close a deal, to cut a deal, to seal a deal, to strike a deal, to work out a deal, to hack out a deal

Hot air
Function: Noun
Meaning: Exaggerated talk
Example: They filed a lawsuit against us despite their flawed arguments. Fortunately the judge recognized that there is a lot of **hot air** in their complaint and ruled in our favor.

Ironclad (to be)
Function: Adjective
Meaning: Describing an unchangeable contract
Example: I'm glad this contract is **ironclad**. It would be devastating if our clients tried to break it after all the negotiations.

Keep/hold one's cards close to one's chest
Function: Verb
Meaning: To be secretive about one's plan or intentions; to be unwilling to share information
Example: Bruce **keeps his cards close to his chest.** He will never tell you what he's thinking.

Knock down one's price

Function: Verb

Meaning: To reduce one's intended price for something

Example: The car salesmen says he'll **knock down the price** of the car by $1000 if I pay in cash.

Synonym: cut back the price, knock off the price

Lay all one's cards on the table

Function: Verb

Meaning: To be entirely open and honest during a negotiation

Example: In the end, the only option was to **lay all my cards on the table** and explain our financial troubles. It was the best way to save time by narrowing down our choices with the right investors.

Let someone walk away with something

Function: Verb

Meaning: To allow someone to have something (with very little effort on their part)

Example: I'll make you a special deal. I'll **let you walk away with** this added bonus if you sign the contract today.

Level playing field

Function: Noun

Meaning: An environment in which all the companies are given an equal ability to compete

Example: We aren't competing on a **level playing field** because our competitors have all been in the market for at least twenty years longer than we have.

Nail down the terms of an agreement

Function: Verb

Meaning: To talk about and make concrete conditions of a contract

Example: We need to **nail down the terms of our contract** so we can clarify what services both parties will offer.

Negotiating table

Function: Noun

Meaning: The location where negotiations are carried out (usually metaphorically speaking)

Example: We must head back to **the negotiating table** and try once again to reach an agreement.

No-win situation

Function: Noun

Meaning: A situation where neither party prevails or benefits

Example: Bob says he's going to quit if he doesn't get a raise. His company really needs him to stay, but they simply can't afford to raise his salary. It's a **no-win situation.**

Off the record
Function: Noun
Meaning: A statement made in confidence and not to be used for publication
Example: I'm going to tell you something confidential, but remember it's **off the record**. The company will be closing its doors in twenty days.

Over a barrel (to have someone)
Function: Verb
Meaning: To place someone in a situation in which he or she has no other choice except to concede to someone else's demands
Example: Our client has us **over a barrel** because he knows we need all the work we can get during this kind of recession.

Play ball
Function: Verb
Meaning: To co-operate with someone (often related to some questionable deals)
Example: I was shocked when my manager told me that if I wanted to keep my job, I needed to **play ball** with him.

Play hardball
Function: Verb
Meaning: To aggressively try to achieve one's aim; to be extremely uncompromising with one's decision during a negotiation
Example: Our client needs to know that we are serious about the conditions of our deal. Therefore, let's **play hardball** and stop catering to all their needs.

Rip-off
Function: Noun
Meaning: A deceiving act or dishonest transaction
Example: We paid for two Broadway show orchestra tickets online but instead received two balcony seats. What a **rip-off!**

Rock-bottom offer
Function: Noun
Meaning: The most reduced price that can be offered
Example: We weren't able to refuse his **rock-bottom offer** because it was too good to miss.

Scab
Function: Noun
Meaning: An offensive name given to a person who replaces an employee who is on strike
Example: When the **scabs** were brought into the factory, the angry employees on the picket line outside were furious to see that the company did that.

See eye to eye
Function: Verb
Meaning: To agree on something
Example: Charlotte and I never **see eye to eye** and that's why we're always angry with each other.
Synonym: *go along with; be on the same wavelength*
Antonym: *bump heads; lock horns*

Sickout
Function: Noun
Meaning: An organized group effort done by employees who pretend to be sick on the same day and do not go to work in order to show management that they are valuable and should be better compensated
Example: Some of the more outspoken employees are trying to organize a **sickout** since management refuses to give us better wages and benefits.

Sit-down strike
Function: Noun
Meaning: A protest in which employees sit on the ground, block the entrance to prevent scabs from replacing them and refuse to leave the workplace until an agreement is reached
Example: The CEO and Board of Directors need to reconsider the budget revisions if they want to avoid a **sit-down strike.**

Sit on the fence
Function: Verb
Meaning: To be hesitant to choose a side or make a decision
Example: Make up your mind which proposal you prefer. Don't **sit on the fence.** We need to make a decision today.

Skirt the issue
Function: Verb
Meaning: To stay away from the topic
Example: The landlord kept **skirting the issue** about when the payment is actually due.

Square deal
Function: Noun
Meaning: A fair, reasonable arrangement
Example: Both parties felt like they got a **square deal** after several days of negotiation. Each party was able to maintain some of their key demands.

Stick to one's guns
Function: Verb
Meaning: To firmly uphold one's conditions or principles
Example: I have to **stick to my guns,** even if I lose that client. I am not willing to offer a twenty percent discount to the client because it's a bad business decision.

Sweeten the deal

Function: Verb

Meaning: To propose something during a negotiation that will be appealing to the other side

Example: As a way to **sweeten the deal**, we will provide your company with free domestic shipping for a month.

Take it or leave it

Function: Verb

Meaning: A common expression used in business negotiations meaning that the opposing party must accept the terms being proposed or else the negotiations will end

Example: I've already lowered my price as far as it can go. This is the absolute final offer. **Take it or leave it.**

Throw in something

Function: Verb

Meaning: To give something away for free as an incentive to get someone's business

Example: I don't usually do this for clients, but if you buy this car right now, I'll **throw in** two tickets for a trip to Hawaii.

Undercut

Function: Verb

Meaning: To offer a lower price than one's competition

Example: We're going to **undercut** the competition and that way we'll make a greater profit.

Synonyms: *underbid, undersell*

"You scratch my back; I'll scratch yours."

Function: Sentence

Meaning: If you do something for me, then I will later repay the favor and do something for you.

Example: I won't report your mistake to the manager if you help me finish my project. **You scratch my back; I'll scratch yours.**

Water under the bridge

Function: Noun phrase

Meaning: Because a past event or mistake happened already, there is no point in mentioning or worrying about it.

Example: Forgot about our disagreement yesterday. It is **water under the bridge**. Instead let's concentrate on the future.

Wheel and deal

Function: Verb

Meaning: To bargain

Example: The negotiators **wheeled and dealed** for hours before coming to a reasonable agreement.

Related: wheeler-dealer

Meaning: a person who bargains well

Win-win situation

Function: Noun

Meaning: A situation in which every person benefits

Example: Working on commission is a **win-win situation** for both the company and me. The more products I sell, the more money the company and I make!

Work someone down

Function: Verb

Meaning: To try and get someone to reduce his or her prices

Example: When you negotiate with Mr. Johnson, try to **work him down**. We simply cannot afford the prices he wants to charge us.

Chapter 4

Expressions By Keyword

4.1 Body-related

4.1.1 Head

Head

Bury one's head in the sand

Come to a head

Count heads/head-counting

Fall/be head over heels in love

Get into one's head

Go to one's head

Have a good head on one's shoulders

Head and shoulders above

Head for

Head-on confrontation

Head start

Hold one's head high

Keep one's head/keep a level head

Keep one's head above water

Keep one's head down

Knock their heads together

Lose one's head

Make headway

Over one's head

Put ideas into someone's head

Put out of one's head

Put their heads together

Scratch one's head

Snap off/bite off someone's head

Head-related expressions - detailed explanations

Bury one's head in the sand
Meaning: To ignore a situation
Example: I realized much about the market had changed once I stopped **burying my head in the sand** and took notice of the US dollar's declining value.

Come to a head
Meaning: To reach a crisis point
Example: As stock continues to decrease in value and more employees are laid off, I worry the company's outdated business plan will **come to a head**.

Count heads/do a head count
Meaning: To count how many people are in a place
Example: We **did a head count** to see how many people had come to the meeting.

Fall/be head over heels in love
Meaning: To be in love with something very suddenly and intensely
Example: As wine connoisseurs, they **fell head over heels in love** with the idea of buying a vineyard.

Get something into one's head
Meaning: To learn; to comprehend something
Example: In order to **get** all the new company policies **into everyone's heads,** there were many mandatory training sessions.

Go to one's head
Meaning: To be made vain or conceited by success
Example: After a few years of owning a successful upstart company, he let things **go to his head** and forgot about all the people who had helped him become a success.

Have a good head on one's shoulders
Meaning: To possess good judgment
Example: Most of my classmates are smart and capable, but my partner for this project **has a good head on his shoulders** and knows exactly what to do.

Head and shoulders above something/someone else
Meaning: To be superior to others
Example: Bob's advanced degree and twenty years of experience in the entertainment industry puts him **head and shoulders above** other applicants that have much less experience.

Head for
Meaning: To move towards (sometimes an undesired result)
Example: Even though that technology company doubled its price on its first day of trading, I can promise you it will be **heading for** a bankruptcy or sale within three years.

Head-on confrontation

Meaning: A strong disagreement with someone whose opinions are completely opposed to one's own

Example: I am afraid a **head-on confrontation** between our two stubborn directors is inevitable. They have never been able to compromise.

Head start

Meaning: An advantage over one's competitors

Example: My friend was worried that his humanities undergraduate program didn't prepare him very well for graduate study in finance, so he decided to get a **head start** by taking a few math classes.

Hold one's head high

Meaning: To be free from guilt; to show that one is not ashamed

Example: Although Jim made some bad investments two years, he has **held his head high** and has now doubled his shares in one of the fastest growing tech companies.

Keep one's head/keep a level head

Meaning: To remain calm and sensible

Example: Despite miscalculating fourth quarter profits and overspending, management **kept a level head** by developing some new strategic plans.

Keep one's head above water

Meaning: To have just enough money to live or to continue a business

Example: With extra revenue from private sponsorship, our non-profit is managing to **keep its head above water.**

Keep one's head down

Meaning: To avoid drawing attention to oneself

Example: Mike tried to **keep his head down** until the end of the year after making that inappropriate comment at the office holiday party.

Knock their heads together

Meaning: To take drastic action to end an argument

Example: If someone doesn't **knock their heads together**, the Board of Trustees and the CEO will never agree on where to take the company in the future.

Lose one's head

Meaning: To act irrational; to lose one's sense of reasoning

Example: Jerry needs to learn how to control himself. He is constantly **losing his head** over the slightest setbacks.

Make headway

Meaning: To make progress on an obstacle; to prevail over a challenge

Example: He **made headway** on the proposal after working many hours of overtime.

Over one's head
Meaning: Intellectually too difficult to grasp
Example: I thought taking a business Chinese language course might be *over my head*, but I discovered I have a natural talent for languages.
Variation: To appeal against the decision of one's immediate superior to someone higher up in the hierarchy
Example: The sales team went *over the head* of the sales manager and pitched their idea directly to the district manager.

Put ideas into someone's head
Meaning: To have an influence (usually a bad influence) on someone
Example: Who *put all these ideas into her head* about becoming an executive when she doesn't even have her MBA?

Put something out of one's head
Meaning: To dismiss something from one's mind
Example: She needs to *put* all her self-doubt *out of her head* before she accepts the promotion from junior to senior manager.

Put your/our/their heads together
Meaning: To collaborate
Example: They work well as partners and usually develop great product ideas when they *put their heads together*.

Scratch one's head
Meaning: To be puzzled or confused
Example: Because I have not taken a math class in many years, I was *scratching my head* throughout the first few sessions of Finance Accounting.

Snap off/bite off someone's head
Meaning: To speak sharply to someone
Example: After coming to work late every day for the past month, he knew his supervisor was going to *bite off his head*.

4.1.2 Hair

<u>**Hair**</u>
Let one's hair down

Split hairs/hair-splitting

Hair-related expressions - detailed explanations

Let one's hair down

Meaning: To relax and enjoy oneself

Example: Once the deal was made, we decided to go out for a drink so everyone could *let their hair down.*

Split hairs/hair-splitting

Meaning: To make insignificant distinctions, to argue with exaggerated subtlety

Example: After revising the report countless times, it no longer made sense to *split hairs* over every single footnote and punctuation mark.

4.1.3 Shoulders

<u>Shoulders</u>

A shoulder to cry on

Carry/have something on one's shoulders

Chip on the shoulder

Give someone the cold shoulder

Put one's shoulder to the wheel

Rub shoulders with

Shoulder out

Shoulder the blame

Shoulder-related expressions - detailed explanations

A shoulder to cry on
Meaning: A good friend; someone you can rely on for comfort in a time of need
Example: Without **a shoulder to cry on**, he became depressed because of all his problems at work.

Carry/have something on one's shoulders
Meaning: To bear responsibility for something
Example: Since I supplied most of of the start-up capital with my own money, I am truly **carrying** the success or failure of this online retail business **on my shoulders.**

Chip on one's shoulder
Meaning: A grievance on one's mind which negatively colors one's attitude
Example: Be wary of making a deal with those clients. They carry on a **chip on their shoulders** after their previous supplier continually gave them damaged goods.

Give someone the cold shoulder
Meaning: To treat someone with marked coldness
Example: We used to talk everyday by the water cooler, but since our dispute last week he has **given me the cold shoulder.**

Put one's shoulder to the wheel
Meaning: To throw all one's energy into a task
Example: Typically Rebecca doesn't exert much effort, but I see that she is **putting her shoulder to the wheel** for this project.

Rub shoulders with someone
Meaning: To spend time with someone socially
Example: The monthly international student club receptions offered a chance for us to **rub shoulders with** people from other countries.

Shoulder out someone
Meaning: To remove someone from a job position
Example: The only way to **shoulder out** Nancy from her current position is to expose her incompetence.

Shoulder the blame
Meaning: To accept full responsibility
Example: Even though we work as a team, our project manager **shouldered the blame** when we did not make our deadline.

4.1.4 Arm

Arm

Arm-twisting

At arm's length

Give one's right arm

With one arm tied behind one's back

Arm-related expressions - detailed explanations

Arm-twisting
Meaning: Threatening, putting pressure on someone
Example: There was no need for **arm-twisting.** When the boss told him he needed to fly to Hawaii on business, he was ready to go immediately!

At arm's length
Meaning: At a distance
Example: I have never trusted Eric, so I keep him **at arm's length** by always declining his suggestions to work together.

Give one's right arm
Meaning: To want something very much
Example: I would **give my right arm** for a cup of coffee right now. I'm so tired.

With one arm tied behind one's back
Meaning: With no difficulty or problem
Example: I know Sara is the best one for the job. Even though she has less experience, she can win over the most demanding clients **with one arm tied behind her back.**

4.1.5   Hand

Hand

Bite the hand that feeds you

Eat out of someone's hand

Hand over fist

In good hands

Right-hand man/woman

Show of hands

Take one's life in one's hands

Hand-related expressions - detailed explanations

Bite the hand that feeds you
Meaning: To harm someone that has been helping you
Example: Tom really **bit the hands that feed us** by treating our best customers so rudely.

Eat out of someone's hand
Meaning: To submit willingly to someone's wishes, to do anything to please someone
Example: Tom is such a smooth-talker that he gets the clients **eating out of his hands** and following all his suggestions easily.

Hand over fist
Meaning: Rapidly in great amounts (usually money)
Example: Bob's new business is doing great – he's really making money **hand over fist**.

In good hands
Meaning: To be cared for, to be well looked after
Example: We need to reassure our clients that they will be **in good hands** with us by providing the best possible customer service.

Right-hand man/woman
Meaning: Someone who is very useful
Example: John is my **right-hand man** at work. I couldn't survive without him!

Show of hands
Meaning: Taking a vote by asking all those who agree with a proposal to raise their hands
Example: A **show of hands** decided which advertising campaign our firm would choose for the new line of products.

Take one's life in one's hands
Meaning: To take a dangerous risk
Example: Talking to the boss when he's in a bad mood is like **taking your life in your hands**. I recommend that you wait until he's not so angry.

4.1.6 Thumb

Thumb

Give something the thumbs down

Thumb through

Twiddle one's thumbs

Stick out like a sore thumb

Thumb-related expressions - detailed explanations

Give something the thumbs down

Meaning: To reject something

Example: I was shocked when my manager *gave my idea the thumbs down*. I was sure he would love it.

Thumb through

Meaning: To turn the pages of a book or look through a pile of papers, usually without reading carefully or purposefully

Example: He *thumbed through* his emails, looking for the one from his contact in France.

Twiddle one's thumbs

Meaning: To be idle, to have nothing to do

Example: Rather than *twiddle her thumbs* during the slow quarter, she used her extra time to start on a creative new proposal.

Stick out like a sore thumb

Meaning: To be conspicuous because of some odd or peculiar feature

Example: As an entry-level employee, Ned tried not to *stick out like a sore thumb* when he was invited to an executive luncheon.

4.1.7 Leg

Leg

Leg-up

On one's/its last legs

Pull someone's leg

Stretch one's legs

Leg-related expressions - detailed explanations

Leg-up
Meaning: A position of advantage; a boost
Example: Studying with that tutor will give you a ***leg-up*** for the exam.

On one's/its last legs
Meaning: To be on the point of collapse, to be worn out
Example: She is ***on her last legs*** after working overtime every night for the past weeks.

Pull someone's leg
Meaning: To play a joke on someone
Example: He has no sense of humor; therefore, you should not try to ***pull his leg***.

Stretch one's legs
Meaning: Stand up or go for a walk, especially after a prolonged period of sitting
Example: Let's ***stretch our legs*** outside during our break from the training session.

4.1.8   Foot

Foot

A foot in both camps

Be on one's feet

Best foot forward

Have/get a foot in the door

Put one's foot down

Start on the wrong foot

Foot-related expressions - detailed explanations

A foot in both camps
Meaning: To be involved with two groups of people who often have very different aims and opinions

Example: He has moved from the non-profit to the corporate world, but he still keeps *a foot in both camps.*

Be on one's feet
Meaning: To stand, usually for an extended period of time

Example: Since she started the new job, Beth is hardly ever *on her feet* because most of the work is done in front of a computer screen.

Best foot forward
Meaning: To do something as well as you can

Example: You won't impress anyone unless you put your *best foot forward.*

Have/get a foot in the door
Meaning: To have/gain access to an opportunity

Example: As a recent graduate lacking a strong networks of contacts, I am finding it difficult to *get my foot in the door* at any top investment firms.

Put one's foot down
Meaning: To impose one's authority; to stop some action of which one disapproves

Example: If you want your boss to take you seriously, *put your foot down* and explain that you can handle more responsibility.

Start on the wrong foot
Meaning: To make a mistake at the very beginning of a relationship or project

Example: I did not want to *start on the wrong foot* at the beginning of the semester, so I devised a schedule for studying.

4.2   Common nouns

4.2.1 Ball

Ball

A ball of fire

Drop the ball

Have the ball at one's feet

Keep the ball rolling

On the ball

Play ball

The ball is in one's court

Ball-related expressions - detailed explanations

A ball of fire
Meaning: A highly energetic or dynamic person
Example: I hope Steve joins our sales team; he is **a real ball of fire** and knows how to open up even the most reserved people.

Drop the ball
Meaning: To make a mistake, especially by doing something in a stupid or careless way
Example: He **dropped the ball** with our clients by showing up for the appointment thirty minutes late.

Have the ball at one's feet
Meaning: To have the opportunity one has been waiting for
Example: All his hard work has paid off and now he **has the ball at his feet.** He earned a scholarship to the school that he hoped for!

Keep the ball rolling
Meaning: To keep the interest alive
Example: In order to **keep the ball rolling**, we should continually ask our clients how we can better serve them.

On the ball
Meaning: Alert; quick
Example: I have been trying to stay **on the ball** by studying for the exam for at least two hours every day.

Play ball
Meaning: To cooperate with
Example: We decided to **play ball** with the other small independent firms in order to compete against the big corporations in this tough market.

The ball is in one's court
Meaning: It is one's turn to take the next step (in a negotiation, dispute)
Example: Since **the ball is in our court**, we must move quickly before losing our chance to buy the franchise from Mr. Brown.

4.2.2 Boat & Sail

<u>Boat</u>

In the same boat

Miss the boat

Rock the boat

<u>Sail</u>

Sail against the wind

Sail into

Sail through

Smooth sailing

Boat-related expressions - detailed explanations

In the same boat
Meaning: To suffer the same predicament as somebody else
Example: All record companies are **in the same boat** trying to cope with the rise of free music downloads.

Miss the boat
Meaning: To miss an important opportunity
Example: Unfortunately, we **missed the boat** when we decided not to join the on-line networking site last year.

Rock the boat
Meaning: To disturb a stable situation
Example: I hate to **rock the boat**, but I do think we need to rewrite this report.

Sailing-related expressions - detailed explanations

Sail against the wind
Meaning: To oppose the prevailing view
Example: He's **sailing against the wind** in his attempt to stop a woman from becoming CEO.

Sail into someone
Meaning: To scold or attack someone
Example: Due to his short temper, he frequently **sails into** his employees when they make minor mistakes.

Sail through
Meaning: To succeed without any difficulty
Example: After a stellar first interview, I hope to **sail through** the second round.

Smooth sailing
Meaning: An easy, uncomplicated plan of action
Example: The first few months of the program were difficult, but I think it's **smooth sailing** from here on.

4.2.3   Cat

<u>Cat</u>
Be catty

Cat-call

Curiosity killed the cat

Grin like a cheshire cat

Let the cat out of the bag

Play cat and mouse

See which way the cat jumps

There's more than one way to kill/skin a cat

Cat-related expressions - detailed explanations

Be catty

Meaning: To make spiteful remarks

Example: After Jane criticized Beth's work, Beth **became catty** and told Jane that her contributions to the team were insignificant.

Cat-call

Meaning: An outcry expressing disapproval

Example: There were **cat-calls** from the audience when the speaker said something that people did not agree with.

Curiosity killed the cat

Meaning: Excessive curiosity can lead one into trouble

Example: **Curiosity killed the cat,** so I'm not going to ask Tom and Bill about the conversation I heard them having.

Grin like a cheshire cat

Meaning: To grin widely from ear to ear

Example: My clients were **grinning like the Cheshire Cat** when they saw the drastic increase in profits last quarter.

Let the cat out of the bag

Meaning: To blurt out a secret

Example: Everyone was angry at Joe after he **let the cat out of the bag** about the surprise party for Susan when she was standing right there.

Play cat and mouse

Meaning: To try to defeat someone by tricking them into making a mistake so that you have an advantage over them

Example: Rather than **play cat and mouse** with his competition, he decided to beat them with simple hard work.

See which way the cat jumps

Meaning: To delay making a decision or doing something until you know what is going to happen or what other people are going to do

Example: You should wait and **see which way the cat jumps** before you give your opinion.

There's more than one way to kill/skin a cat

Meaning: There is more than one method for achieving a goal; there are always alternative methods

Example: If our first proposal is rejected, there is no need to panic. We can use our backup. **There's more than one way to kill a cat.**

4.2.4 Colors

Colors
Bright/dark

Color of someone's money

Colorless

Give/lend color to

Have one's views colored by

Off color

Rose-colored/rose-tinted spectacles

True colors/to show one's true colors

With flying colors

Win one's colors

Color-related expressions - detailed explanations

Bright/dark

Meaning: To describe something in a favorable or unfavorable way

Example: He is sure to have a **bright** future with a degree from a top-tiered school.

Example: His future looks **dark** now that he has dropped out of school.

Color of someone's money

Meaning: To prove that you can pay for something

Example: Before we proceed with negotiations and invest more time in the deal, let's see the **color of your money**.

Colorless

Meaning: To lack personality; uninteresting

Example: The new hire is completely **colorless.** He never laughs at any of our office antics and never ventures far from his desk.

Give/lend color to

Meaning: To make something (a story, explanation, etc.) more credible or plausible

Example: She **gave color to** her proposal by citing specific examples from other companies that used similar business plans.

Have one's views colored by something

Meaning: To have one's ideas and opinions heavily influenced by external forces

Example: His view's of running a business have been **colored by** his extensive travels to other parts of the world.

Off color

Meaning: Not decent or proper

Example: Some of his jokes were a little **off-color** and I don't think our co-workers particularly appreciated them.

Rose-colored/rose-tinted glasses

Meaning: To see things in a falsely flattering or over-optimistic light

Example: Eventually she will need to take off her **rose-colored** glasses and see that most people do not have altruistic motives.

True colors/to show one's true colors

Meaning: To reveal one's true self

Example: It is essential to **show your true colors** during your admissions interview in order to give the interviewer a genuine image of yourself.

With flying colors

Meaning: With great success

Example: Michael passed the test **with flying colors** and scored in the 99th percentile.

Win one's colors

Meaning: To win recognition for one's achievements

Example: If you want to **win your colors**, strengthen your visibility in the workplace with effective verbal communication.

4.2.5 Feather

<u>Feather</u>

Birds of a feather

In fine feather

Smooth someone's ruffled feathers

You could have knocked me down with a feather!

Feather-related expressions - detailed explanations

Birds of a feather

Meaning: People of the same character associate with one another

Example: I already know that he will deny my proposal to update the system. He is a member of the old-fashioned management team – they're all ***birds of a feather***.

In fine feather

Meaning: In splendid condition, lively and cheerful

Example: He was ***in fine feather*** for weeks after getting the promotion.

Smooth someone's ruffled feathers

Meaning: To soothe someone's injured pride

Example: After he was waitlisted at his top school, I tried to ***smooth his feathers*** by reminding him that his interview will surely give him an advantage.

You could have knocked me down with a feather!

Meaning: To be completely overcome with surprise

Example: When Paul announced his retirement, ***you could have knocked me down with a feather***! He is only thirty-five years old!

4.2.6 Leaf

<u>**Leaf**</u>
Leaf through

Read the tea leaves

Shake like a leaf

Take a leaf out of someone's book

Turn over a new leaf

Leaf-related expressions - detailed explanations

Leaf through
Meaning: To turn the pages of a book without reading it thoroughly, in order to get a general idea of what it is about

Example: Send me the brochure and let me **leaf through** your company profile before setting up a meeting.

Read the tea leaves
Meaning: To foretell someone's future by examining the tea-leaves at the bottom of a cup

Example: I don't need to **read the tea leaves** to know that this candidate is the best one for the position. I already can see he will be successful with us.

Shake like a leaf
Meaning: To tremble with fear

Example: Because of his fear of public speaking, Michael was **shaking like a leaf** before talking to hundreds of attendees at the national conference.

Take a leaf out of someone's book
Meaning: To follow someone's example

Example: I would never **take a leaf out of his book.** He is a terrible mentor.

Turn over a new leaf
Meaning: To make a fresh start

Example: After getting fired from a public relations firm, he wanted to **turn over a new leaf.** He decided to go to business school to further his career opportunities.

Chapter 5

Sports Related Expressions

5.1 General

A good/bad sport

Blow the whistle on someone

Bounce something off someone

Get the ball rolling

Hard to call

Play by the rules/play fair

Score points / score big

Team player

Time out!

General sports-related expressions - detailed explanations

A good/bad sport

Meaning: One who is cooperative (a good sport) or uncooperative (a bad sport) in carrying out an unpleasant assignment

Example: I know you're not happy with your new work task, but you shouldn't be *a bad sport* about it.

Related: *To be a sport* (similar to "to be a good sport")

Blow the whistle on someone

Meaning: To report someone's inappropriate or illegal actions

Example: After Bill *blew the whistle on his company's president,* all the major newspapers wanted to interview him.

Related: *Whistle-blower*

Bounce something off someone

Meaning: To share an idea or proposal with someone in order to get feedback

Example: Can I talk to you for a minute? I want to *bounce an idea off you.*

Get the ball rolling

Meaning: To start a task

Example: Susan was eager to *get the ball rolling* with her new assignment.

Hard to call

Meaning: Difficult to determine

Example: Because we don't have final sales figures, it's *hard to call* the success of our campaign.

Play by the rules/play fair

Meaning: To behave in a fair and honest way

Example: That manager doesn't have the respect of his employees because he never *plays by the rules.*

Score points / score big

Meaning: To earn someone's favor

Example: Robert *scored points* with the boss by complimenting his golf skills.

Team player

Meaning: One who works well with other members of their organization to attain a goal

Example: I really don't like working with Jim because he isn't a very good *team player*

Time out!

Meaning: To take a break due to fatigue or an unexpected turn of events

Example: After two hours of little progress during the meeting, the leader called *time out* so everyone could clear their minds.

5.1.1 Baseball

<u>**Baseball**</u>
Bat a thousand

Come out of left field

Drop the ball

Field a phone call

Go to bat for someone

Hit a home run

In the same league as someone or something

Keep one's eye on the ball

Make it to first base

Off base

Out of someone's league

Pinch hit

Pitch ideas

Play hardball

Strike out

Take a rain check

That's one strike (against someone)

Throw someone a curveball

To be home free

To be in the ball park

Touch base with someone

Baseball-related expressions - detailed explanations

Bat a thousand
Meaning: To perform extremely well - even perfectly - at a task
Example: Everything is going so well for me. I feel like I'm **batting a thousand** today!

Come out of left field
Meaning: To be unexpected, and possibly unusual
Example: Bob really surprised everyone during the meeting. He **came out of left field** with a new idea.

Drop the ball
Meaning: To make a mistake, often due to carelessness
Example: I **dropped the ball** when I missed my meeting with our client.

Field a phone call
Meaning: To answer a phone call
Example: I've been busy all morning **fielding phone calls** from new customers.

Go to bat for someone
Meaning: To provide support for another by taking on responsibilities or requesting a favor on their behalf
Example: Bill **went to bat for** Susan when she needed someone to talk to the boss about her getting a raise.

Hit a home run
Meaning: To perform in a particularly successful manner
Example: Frank **hit a home run** with his new business proposal. Everyone loves it!

In the same league as someone (or something)
Meaning: To possess similar qualifications or achievements to someone or something else
Example: I tried playing golf with Fred, but I'm just not **in the same league as** him. I think I should take some lessons.

Keep one's eye on the ball
Meaning: To pay careful attention to an objective
Example: Whenever I get discouraged about my efforts, my coworker tells me to **keep my eye on the ball** and that advice really helps.

Make it to first base
Meaning: To successfully take the initial step towards an objective
Example: Though I haven't risen very far in this company yet, I feel like I've **made it to first base** by getting a job here.

Off base
Meaning: To be wrong or disrespectful
Example: I think your claims about him are **off base.**

Out of someone's league
Meaning: Not possessing similar qualifications to someone else; or something is too expensive for a person
Example: I'd like to buy a fancy sports car, but I think that's **out of my league** right now.

Pinch hit
Meaning: To take the place of someone else due to lack of ability
Example: When Bill made a mistake during the presentation, Bob was sent in to **pinch hit** and fix the situation.

Pitch ideas
Meaning: To offer one's ideas
Example: Everyone gathered together to **pitch ideas** on how to improve sales figures.

Play hardball
Meaning: To act in an aggressive manner; to use every means at one's disposal to attain a goal
Example: When the smaller company resisted being bought out, the big corporation decided to **play hardball** in order to get what they wanted.

Strike out
Meaning: To fail
Example: We thought our proposal was a good one, but we **struck out** with our clients.

Take a rain check
Meaning: To postpone until a later date
Example: Steve was too busy to meet his friend for a drink, so he asked to **take a rain check.**

That's one strike (against someone)
Meaning: One mistake out of three mistakes allowed in total (Two strikes against someone. Three strikes and you are out!)
Example: The new employee was late on his first day. **That's one strike against him.**

Throw someone a curveball
Meaning: To surprise someone with something difficult or unexpected
Example: Just as I was getting ready to go on vacation, my boss **threw me a curve ball** and told me he needed me to work this weekend.

To be home free
Meaning: To be without encumbrances
Example: As soon as I finish this report, I **am home free** and can relax.

To be in the ball park

Meaning: To be in the vicinity of a desired target.

Example: Bob is selling his home, but all incoming offers are not even *in the ball park* of what he expects.

Related: *ballpark figure* (an estimated number)

Touch base with someone

Meaning: To contact someone

Example: I ended the phone call by saying I would *touch base* with the client next week.

5.1.2 Swimming

Swimming
Dive right in

Drowning in something

Get one's feet wet

Go in headfirst

In deep water

Jump off the deep end

Sink or swim

Test the water

Swimming-related expressions - detailed explanations

Dive right in

Meaning: To start immediately without hesitation

Example: When Dan has a new project, he likes to **dive right in.**

Drowning in something

Meaning: To be overwhelmed by something

Example: Some people use credit unwisely, and soon they are **drowning in debit.**

Get one's feet wet

Meaning: To begin something for the first time

Example: Susan **got her feet wet** after finishing college by going to work at her uncle's business.

Go in headfirst

Meaning: To begin something heedlessly without considering the consequences

Example: Bob's style is to **go in headfirst,** but it often gets him in trouble.

Go off the deep end

Meaning: To become so angry that one loses control of their emotions

Example: My wife **went off the deep end** when I forgot her birthday.

In deep water

Meaning: To be in a difficult or troubling situation

Example: I realized I was **in deep water,** and so I asked a coworker for help.

Sink or swim

Meaning: To be in a situation where a great deal of effort is necessary to succeed, otherwise one faces failure

Example: In today's economy, it's really a matter of **sink or swim.**

Test the water

Meaning: To judge reactions to one's ideas or plans in advance; to determine whether something will succeed before advancing

Example: Steve **tested the water** for his proposal by talking first to his manager, and then later going to the owner of his company.

5.1.3 Track and field

<u>Track and field</u>

Clear a hurdle

Come in a close second

Have the inside track

Jump the gun

Keep pace with someone (or something)

Pace oneself

Set the pace

Track and field related expressions - detailed explanations

Clear a hurdle

Meaning: To overcome a difficult obstacle, sometimes one of many

Example: After I **cleared the hurdle** of getting approval for the project, I moved on to the next step.

Come in a close second

Meaning: To narrowly miss being chosen as the first choice for something

Example: Though we worked extremely hard, in the end we **came in a close second**.

Have the inside track

Meaning: To possess the quickest or most effective route to accomplish something; to hold the advantage

Example: Because of Bill's past work experience with ABC Company, we **have the inside track** on how they operate.

Jump the gun

Meaning: To begin prematurely

Example: Let's not **jump the gun** with our actions. Let's stop and think for a moment instead.

Keep pace with someone (or something)

Meaning: To maintain the same level of achievement or competitiveness as someone or something else; to stay up-to-date

Example: To be competitive in this market, we have to **keep pace** with new developments.

Pace oneself

Meaning: To avoid overworking one's self, often to maintain a consistent rate of work

Example: It's a good idea to **pace yourself** on a project, or you risk burning out too soon.

Set the pace

Meaning: To establish the tempo at which others will work; to create a standard

Example: Bob **set the pace** for how he wanted the task to be carried out.

5.1.4 Boating

Boating

Each/every man for himself

Go down with the ship

On an even keel

Rough seas ahead

Smooth sailing

To shape up or ship out

To take the wind out of one's sails

Boating-related expressions - detailed explanations

Each/every man for himself

Meaning: Every person must look out for his or her own self-interest

Example: When the company went bankrupt, it was a case of ***each man for himself*** as people figured out where to go next.

Go down with the ship

Meaning: To stay with a project or organization even though it is failing

Example: Bob decided to quit rather than ***go down with the ship*** when his organization began to fail.

To shape up or ship out

Meaning: To conform to company regulations or improve one's work habits, otherwise face dismissal

Example: The first time Sam was late for a meeting with the boss, he was told to ***shape up or ship out.***

On an even keel

Meaning: To maintain stable performance; to be balanced and certain

Example: After a difficult start with his new job, Donald finally feels like he is ***on an even keel.***

Rough seas ahead

Meaning: To have difficult or demanding challenges in the near future

Example: When management told us we'd have to take a pay cut, we knew there were ***rough seas ahead.***

Smooth sailing

Meaning: A lack of challenges or obstacles

Example: We just need to get through a couple of difficult tasks, and then it will be ***smooth sailing.***

To take the wind out of one's sails

Meaning: To lose one's enthusiasm because of discouragement

Example: The news about budget cuts really ***took the wind out of my sails*** about our new project.

5.1.5 Boxing

Boxing

A heavyweight

A lightweight

To go a few rounds with someone

To hit below the belt

To throw in the towel

Boxing-related expressions - detailed explanations

A heavyweight
Meaning: An esteemed and powerful individual who often holds a high position within an organization

Example: The owner of our business is a real **heavyweight** in the industry. When he talks, everyone listens.

A lightweight
Meaning: One who falters under pressure; one who holds a low position within an organization

Example: If you want to get ahead in this business, you need to stop being **a lightweight.**

To go a few rounds with someone
Meaning: To fight with someone

Example: I **went a few rounds with** Dan about his decision, but in the end we came to an understanding.

To hit (someone) below the belt
Meaning: To harm someone in an unfair or cruel manner

Example: I was shocked to hear about how Fred **hit Bill below the belt.** I didn't expect that kind of behavior from him.

To throw in the towel
Meaning: To give-up, often due to overwhelming difficulty

Example: If one more thing goes wrong today, I will **throw in the towel** and just go home.

5.1.6 American football

American football
Game plan

Huddle

Make a fumble

Run interference for someone

Tackle a problem

Take the ball and run with it

American football related expressions - detailed explanations

Game plan
Meaning: A plan of action or strategy for accomplishing something
Example: If we want to succeed, we had better think of a good *game plan.*

Huddle
Meaning: To have a private team meeting
Example: Bill called the members of his sales team in for a *huddle* before they presented their proposal.

Make a fumble
Meaning: To make a mistake, often due to carelessness
Example: When you *make a fumble,* the most important thing is to fix it and move on.

Run interference for someone
Meaning: To intercept or divert a potential problem for someone else
Example: I *ran interference* for Tom when he became overwhelmed by all of his tasks.

Tackle a problem
Meaning: To solve a problem, especially with vigor
Example: The first step in *tackling a problem* is realizing there is one.

Take the ball and run with it
Meaning: To proceed with an idea or concept; to carry out something
Example: My manager likes to introduce a project, and then she lets us *take the ball and run with it.*

5.1.7 Horse-racing

Horse-racing

Down to the wire

First out of the gate

In the homestretch

In the running

Jockey for position

Neck and neck

Off and running

Out of the running

Right out of the chute

To be left at the gate

Win by a nose

Horse-racing related expressions - detailed explanations

Down to the wire
Meaning: To leave something until the last minute
Example: Bob had to stay late to finish his work because he had left it **down to the wire.**

First out of the gate
Meaning: To be the first to start something; to possess an early advantage
Example: Susan likes to be **first out of the gate** on any project she's involved in.

In the homestretch
Meaning: To be close to finishing something
Example: I'm not completely finished this report, but I am **in the homestretch.**

In the running
Meaning: To be in a favorable position to achieve or win something
Example: Both Bill and Susan are **in the running** for a promotion in our office.

Jockey for position
Meaning: To maneuver into a more favorable position
Example: I think too many people are involved in the project, and everyone is trying to **jockey for position.**

Neck and neck
Meaning: To be even with someone (or something)
Example: Dan and I were **neck and neck** for the sales award, but in the end he was the person to win it.

Off and running
Meaning: To get a good start
Example: It looks like the new team is **off and running** with their assignment.

Out of the running
Meaning: Not likely to achieve or win something
Example: Because of our poor results, my sales team is **out of the running** for a bonus.

Right out of the chute
Meaning: At the very beginning
Example: I knew today was going to be a bad day **right out of the chute.** I should have stayed in bed!

To be left at the gate
Meaning: To be unable to keep up; to be left behind
Example: If you don't work hard in this business, you will **be left at the gate.**

Win by a nose
Meaning: To win by a small amount
Example: At the company picnic, my team did their best during the relay race and **won by a nose.**

Chapter 6

Grammar Review

6.1 Verbs

6.1.1 Major Tenses

A quick review of the tenses and their respective meanings will help you make sense of what can be a confusing topic.

Tense	Example
Simple Present (action frequently happening in the present)	**He laughs.** **They laugh.**
Perfect Progressive (action ongoing at this moment)	He is laughing. They are laughing.
Present Perfect (action started previously and completed thus far)	**He has laughed.** **They have laughed.**
Simple Past (completed action)	**He laughed.** **They laughed.**
Present Perfect Progressive (action started previously and ongoing at this moment)	He has been laughing. They have been laughing.
Past Perfect (action completed before another past time)	**He had laughed.** **They had laughed.**
Future (action to occur later)	**He will laugh.** **They will laugh.**
Future Progressive (action ongoing at a future time)	He will be laughing. They will be laughing.
Future Perfect (action regarded as completed at a future time)	**He will have laughed.** **They will have laughed.**
Future Perfect Progressive (action started at a future time and ongoing)	He will have been laughing. They will have been laughing.

Unfortunately, the rules governing sequence of tenses are a bit of a jumble. Often you will have to rely on your ear and common sense to guide you with these questions. Below are some guidelines you can use in order to decide what the correct sentence should look like. In complex sentences, the tense of the verb in the main clause governs the tenses of the verbs in subsequent or dependent clauses.

Tense in Main Clause	Purpose of Dependent Clause	Tense In Dependent Clause	Example
Present	To show same-time action	Simple Present	**I am eager to go for a walk because I enjoy exercise.**
-	To show earlier action	Simple Past	**He feels that she made a mistake last year.**
-	To show a period of time extending from some point in the past to the present	Present Perfect	**The congregation believes that it has selected a suitable preacher.**
-	To show action to come	Future	**My teacher says that he will grade the test next week.**
Simple Past	To show another completed past action	Simple Past	**She cooked the salmon because she knew it was fresh.**
-	To show an earlier action	Past Perfect	**He cooked the salmon well because he had attended culinary school.**
-	To state a general truth	Simple Present	**Copernicus believed that the universe is like a giant clock.**
Present Perfect	To show an earlier action	Simple Past	**The lawyer has handled many cases since he passed the bar.**
-	To show action happening at the same time	Present Perfect	**She has grown a foot because she has taken steroids.**
Past Perfect	To show completed action in the past	Simple Past	**The bird had flown for miles before it landed.**
Future	To show action happening at the same time	Simple Present	**I will be a senator if they vote for me.**
-	To show an earlier action	Simple Past	**You will pass the test if you studied.**
-	To show future action earlier than the action of the independent clause	Present Perfect	**My grandmother will finish the puzzle soon if her dog has not eaten the pieces.**
Future Perfect	For any purpose	Simple Present	**The factory will have produced many widgets long before it closes.**

6.1.2   List of Irregular Verbs

To correctly use the verbs in different tense forms, please study the list carefully.

Base Form	Past Tense	Past Participle
Awake	Awaked; awoke	Awaked; awoken
Be	Was/Were	Been
Beat	Beat	Beat; beaten
Become	Became	Become
Begin	Began	Begun
Bend	Bent	Bent
Bite	Bit	Bitten
Bleed	Bled	Bled
Blow	Blew	Blown
Break	Broke	Broken
Bring	Brought	Brought
Build	Built	Built
Burst	Burst	Burst
Buy	Bought	Bought
Catch	Caught	Caught
Choose	Chose	Chosen
Come	Came	Come
Cost	Cost	Cost
Cut	Cut	Cut
Deal	Dealt	Dealt
Dig	Dug	Dug
Dive	Dived; dove	Dived
Do	Did	Done
Draw	Drew	Drawn
Dream	Dreamed; dreamt	Dreamed; dreamt
Drink	Drank	Drunk
Drive	Drove	Driven
Eat	Ate	Eaten
Fall	Fell	Fallen
Feed	Fed	Fed
Feel	Felt	Felt
Fight	Fought	Fought
Find	Found	Found
Fit	Fitted; fit	Fitted; fit

Base Form	Past Tense	Past Participle
Fly	Flew	Flown
Forget	Forgot	Forgotten
Freeze	Froze	Frozen
Get	Got	Gotten; got
Give	Gave	Given
Go	Went	Gone
Grow	Grew	Grown
Hang (an object)	Hung	Hung
Hang (a person)	Hanged	Hanged
Hear	Heard	Heard
Hide	Hid	Hidden; hid
Hit	Hit	Hit
Hold	Held	Held
Hurt	Hurt	Hurt
Keep	Kept	Kept
Kneel	Knelt; kneeled	Knelt; kneeled
Knit	Knit; knitted	Knit; knitted
Know	Knew	Known
Lay (put down)	Laid	Laid
Lead	Led	Led
Lean	Leaned	Leaned
Leave	Left	Left
Lend	Lent	Lent
Let	Let	Let
Lie (recline)	Lay	Lain
Lie (speak an untruth)	Lied	Lied
Light	Lighted; lit	Lighted; lit
Lose	Lost	Lost
Make	Made	Made
Mean	Meant	Meant
Meet	Met	Met
Pay	Paid	Paid
Prove	Proved	Proved; proven
Put	Put	Put
Quit	Quit	Quit
Read	Read	Read
Rid	Rid; ridden	Rid; ridden

Base Form	Past Tense	Past Participle
Ride	Rode	Ridden
Ring	Rang	Rung
Run	Ran	Run
Say	Said	Said
See	Saw	Seen
Sell	Sold	Sold
Send	Sent	Sent
Set	Set	Set
Shake	Shook	Shaken
Shine	Shone; shined	Shone; shined
Shoot	Shot	Shot
Show	Showed	Showed; shown
Shrink	Shrank	Shrunk
Shut	Shut	Shut
Sit	Sat	Sat
Sleep	Slept	Slept
Slide	Slid	Slid
Speak	Spoke	Spoken
Speed	Sped; speeded	Sped; speeded
Spend	Spent	Spent
Spin	Spun	Spun
Spring	Sprang	Sprung
Stand	Stood	Stood
Steal	Stole	Stolen
Stick	Stuck	Stuck
Sting	Stung	Stung
Strike	Struck	Struck; stricken
Swear	Swore	Sworn
Swim	Swam	Swum
Swing	Swung	Swung
Take	Took	Taken
Teach	Taught	Taught
Tear	Tore	Torn
Tell	Told	Told
Think	Thought	Thought
Throw	Threw	Thrown
Wake	Waked; woke	Waked; woken
Wear	Wore	Worn
Win	Won	Won
Wring	Wrung	Wrung
Write	Wrote	Written

6.1.3   American vs. British Usage

American spelling often differs from British usage. Examples include:

- The use of *-or* instead of British *-our*, e.g., *color, harbor, favor*, and the use of *-er* for *-re*, e.g., *center, fiber, theater*.

- The final or internal *e* is dropped in *ax, acknowledgment, judgment, jewelry*. Other modifications include: *plow, wagon, check* (cheque), *pajamas, gray, mold, program, draft, marvelous, traveler*.

- The double *-ll* is retained in *skillful, fulfill, install*; the endings *-ise, -isation*, are written, *-ize, -zation*.

Standard American words frequently differ from their British equivalents -

Frequently Used in America	Frequently Used in Britain
apartment	flat
boardwalk	promenade
bug	insect
drapes	curtains
elevator	lift
fall	autumn
fix a flat	change a tire
garbage can	dustbin
gas	petrol
hardware store	ironmonger's
mad	angry
peek	peer, glimpse
pillow	cushion
pitcher	jug
railroad	railway
round trip	return trip
salesgirl	shop assistant
sidewalk	pavement
sick	ill
smokestack	chimney

Chapter 7

Grammar Specifics - Use of Articles

7.1 Guidelines

There are no hard and fast rules about using articles accurately. For many language learners, it can be confusing and frustrating to try to decide how to use these small words. The good news is that errors with articles are not likely to cause you any problems in business.

Even so, it's important to note that correct use of articles will make your English smoother. To help you improve your grammar, we have summarized some basic rules about articles for your easy reference.

#1. No article is necessary before an uncountable noun which is used in an indefinite sense, i.e., in a non-unique, non-specific and non-defined way.

Example: Some people prefer **water** to coffee every morning.
"The" is necessary before an uncountable noun which is used in a definite sense.

Example: **The water** in this town is famous for its purity.
Never use "a" or "an" before an uncountable noun.

Example (incorrect): a happiness
#2. No article is necessary before a plural noun which is used in an indefinite sense.

Example A: Do you have siblings?
Example B: There are stars in the sky.
#3. No article is necessary before the names of streets, avenues, roads, lanes, or boulevards.

Example: I live on Eighth Ave. We are on Main Street.
#4. No "the" is necessary after "some, most, all, many, much, and there is/are". But "the" is necessary if preceded by "some of, most of, all of, many of, much of". Prepositional phrases with "of" makes a noun definite. Therefore "the" is used.

Example: **Many people** showed up yesterday. **Many of the people** I know showed up yesterday.

Final notes:
#1. Depending on the phrase and the meaning, the same noun can be countable in some situations and uncountable in others.

Example A: Our helicopter is running out of **fuel**. Gas is **a fuel** made from petroleum.
Example B: My sister loves **cheese**. Brie is **a** soft and rich French **cheese**.
Example C: **Time** is precious. We had **a wonderful time** at the holiday party.
#2. Indefinite use of a noun includes the following situations:

a) The noun was used as a generic reference
b) The noun was not mentioned before in the context
c) The noun was not known to the speaker as a particular item
d) The noun was not part of a phrase
e) The noun was not defined by a phrase or clause.

7.2   Streets

Are these sentences correct?
I live on the Ninth Street.
I live on the Broadway.
I live on the Cherry Lane.
I live on the main street.
I live on the Main Street.
I saw a Broadway play last week.
A Broadway play that we saw was really amazing.
Please fill in the blanks when applicable. Use a/an/the.
1. Cross _____ Thirteenth Avenue and turn right on _____ Cherry.
2. Mr. Jones lived on _____ Sierra Nevada Lane which is _____ main street in that town.
3. I can't recall the exact name of _____ street that she used to live on.
4. There's _____ road in front of my house.
5. Do _____ Broadway and _____ 116th Street run into each other?
6. _____ off-Broadway show that your mom mentioned was excellent.
7. _____ Fifth Avenue plastic surgeon can charge over 3,000 dollars for the consultation fee.
8. We stopped in Philadelphia to see _____ South Street jazz band.
9. Mr. Jerry is the proprietor of _____ Broadway restaurant where I used to have a job.

7.3   Educational Institutions

What is the rule?
Those students attend Columbia University in Manhattan.
Those students attend the University of Columbia in Bogota.
Please fill in the blanks when applicable.
1. _____ Williams College is in the State of Massachusetts.
2. _____ U of EA is in England.
3. _____ Bowdoin College is located in Maine.
4. Professor Williamson works in _____ College of Arts and Sciences.
5. _____ Nanjing University is in Nanjing, China.
6. I work at biology station for _____ University of Chicago.
7. _____ Pennsylvania State University and _____ University of Pennsylvania are two different schools.
8. _____ Yale School of Management of _____ Yale University has a focus on educating leaders in both public and private sectors.

7.4   Countries, Cities, States

When do you use "the"?
When do you *not* use "the"?

Please fill in the blanks when applicable.

1. The capital of _____ Italy is _____Rome.
2. _____ New Jersey is a state on the east coast of the US.
3. _____ Wales is a part of _____ United Kingdom.
4. _____ Scotland is a part of _____ Great Britain.
5. Puerto Rico is not a city in _____ Mexico!
6. How long have you lived in _____ United States?
7. _____ U.S.S.R. no longer exists.
8. How long have you live in _____ America?
9. There's a song about _____ Chicago, which is also called _____ windy city.
10. My car was made in _____ U.S.A.
11. _____ Canada is not the largest country in the world, but it's much bigger than _____ Kingdom of Morocco, which is south of _____ Spain.
12. Should I say _____ People's Republic of China or just _____ China?

Use a/an/the/0 as required
Cassie's Dilemma

Cassie LaLonde has (a)_____ decision to make. She is (b)_____ French student, and two different universities have offered her a place to study in their colleges of music: (c)_____ University of Midfield in (d)_____ United States and (e)_____ Oxford University in England. She has always dreamed of visiting (f)_____ North America, and she has already seen (g)_____ British Isles many times. However, her cousin lives in (h)_____ England, and she can room with him and cut costs on rent. She also has (i)_____ cousin who goes to (j)_____ Cambridge. She knows that (k)_____ Midfield is (l)_____ famous place for music, but she doesn't think that (m)_____ University of Midfield is as prestigious as (n)_____ Oxford University. This is why Cassie can't make up her mind between going to (o)_____ US or (p)_____ UK.

7.5 Buildings, Geographical Features and More

Use *the* with	- the names of rivers, oceans, seas, and deserts
	- plural names
	- plural of nationalities (which have no other plural form)
	- the names of hotels, motels, theaters, bridges, and buildings
	- the names of zoos, gardens, museums, institutes, and companies
	- when the noun is the only one that exists
Do **not** use *the* with	- the names of single lakes, mountains, islands, or canyons (except "The Grand Canyon")
	- the names of hospitals or halls
	- the names of stadiums, malls, or parks

Please fill in the blanks when applicable.

1. _____ Beacon is a famous New York theater.
2. Do you think _____ Americans are more talkative than _____British?
3. Do you know why _____ sky is blue?
4. That is _____ Caribbean island.
5. _____ Hanging Gardens of Babylon were famous throughout the ancient world.

6. Is this your first time in _____ Uris Hall?
7. _____ Natural History Museum is located on West 81st Street.
8. No pedestrians are allowed to cross _____ Queensboro Bridge.
9. _____Koreans share a border with _____ Chinese.
10. _____New York Presbyterian Hospital has a good reputation.
11. Our galaxy is one of many in _____ universe.
12. _____ Wombat Canyon is a dangerous place to go.
13. Who wouldn't like to sail to _____ Caribbean?
14. _____ Hotel California is mentioned in a well-known song.
15. One of the most scenic rivers in this area is _____ Hudson.
16. The conference will be held at _____ Westin.
17. _____ Nile is one of the longest rivers on earth.
18. _____ Tonga is an island located in _____ Pacific Ocean.
19. Henry Ford founded _____ Ford Motor Company.
20. _____ Japanese are famous for their food.
21. One place to go shopping is _____ Manhattan Mall, which is located on _____Sixth Avenue and _____ 32nd Street.
22. _____ General Motors is a competitor of _____ Ford Motor Company.
23. _____ Sahara Desert is located in Africa.
24. The Sheridan is a boat that travels _____ Atlantic.
25. Mr. Jones was the pilot of _____ Missouri River steamboat.
26. I am not sure if I prefer _____ Shea Stadium as it is now or _____ old Shea Stadium.
27. _____ Bronx Zoo has so many different kinds of mammals.
28. Have you ever been to _____ Lake Superior or _____ Mt. Everest?

7.6 Few vs. a Few & Little vs. a Little

What is the difference in meaning in these sentences?
I have *a few* friends.
I have *few* friends.
I have *a little* energy.
I have *little* energy.
Use nouns such as *money, time, friend, experience, memory, gas, change, sympathy, information, pollution, people, kid, class, idea* to complete the sentences below. For each sentence, use either a few/a little or few/little.
1. I had a hard childhood so I _____.
2. I'm so broke! I _____.
3. Only after I turned on the engine did I realize that the car _____.
4. After she failed out of college, her parents _____.
5. She is never lonely because _____.
6. Whenever I think about traveling to a new place, I realize that I _____.
7. Whenever I think about writing my dissertation, I feel so nervous because I _____.
Use your own ideas to write the following sentences.
1. Write two sentences.

a. (little water)
b. (a little water)

2. Write two sentences.
a. (few languages)
b. (a few languages)

7.7 ANSWER KEY

9.2 Streets
Are these sentences correct?

I live on the Ninth Street.	*incorrect*	(correct sentence: I live on Ninth Street.)
I live on the Broadway.	*incorrect*	(correct sentence: I live on Broadway.)
I live on the Cherry Lane.	*incorrect*	(correct sentence: I live on Cherry Lane.)
I live on the main street.	*correct*	
I live on the Main Street.	*incorrect*	(correct sentence: I live on Main Street.)

I saw a Broadway play last week.   *correct*
A Broadway play that we saw was really amazing.   *incorrect*
(correct sentence: The Broadway play that we saw was really amazing.)
Correct Sentences:
1. Cross Thirteenth Avenue and turn right on Cherry.
2. Mr. Jones lived on Sierra Nevada Lane which is **the** main street in that town.
3. I can't recall the exact name of **the** street that she used to live on.
4. There's **a** road in front of my house.
5. Do Broadway and 116th Street run into each other?
6. The off-Broadway show that your mom mentioned was excellent.
7. **A** Fifth Avenue plastic surgeon can charge over 3,000 dollars for the consultation fee.
8. We stopped in Philadelphia to see **the** South Street jazz band.
8. Mr. Jerry is the proprietor of **the** Broadway restaurant where I used to have a job.

9.3 Educational Institutions
What is the rule?
Use "the" if "of" appears in the name of the university.
Correct Sentences:
1. Williams College is in the State of Massachusetts.
2. The U of EA is in England.
3. Bowdoin College is located in Maine.
4. Professor Williamson works in the College of Arts and Sciences.
5. Nanjing University is in Nanjing, China.
6. I work at biology station for the University of Chicago.
7. Pennsylvania State University and the University of Pennsylvania are two different schools.
8. The Yale School of Management of Yale University has a focus on educating leaders in both public and private sectors.

9.4 Countries, Cities, States
When do you use "the"?
Use "the" if the country's name includes "union," "united," "republic," or "kingdom" in the title, even if the country's name is abbreviated with letters. Also use "the" if the country is plural (ending in "s").
When do you not use "the"?
Omit "the" for all other countries.
Correct Sentences:
1. The capital of Italy is Rome.
2. New Jersey is a state on the east coast of the US.
3. Wales is a part of **the** United Kingdom.
4. Scotland is a part of Great Britain.
5. Puerto Rico is not a city in Mexico!
6. How long have you lived in **the** United States?
7. **The** U.S.S.R. no longer exists.
8. How long have you lived in America?
9. There's a song about Chicago, which is also called **The** Windy City.
10. My car was made in **the** U.S.A.
11. Canada is not the largest country in the world, but it's much bigger than **the** Kingdom of Morocco, which is south of Spain.
12. Should I say **the** People's Republic of China or just China?

Cassie's Dilemma

(a) **a**	(b) **a**	(c) **the**	(d) **the**	(e) –
(f) –	(g) **the**	(h) –	(i) **a**	(j) –
(k) –	(l) **a**	(m) **the**	(n) –	(o) **the**
(p) **the**				

9.5 Buildings, Geographical Features and More
Correct Sentences:
1. **The** Beacon is a famous New York theater.
2. Do you think Americans are more talkative than **the** British?
3. Do you know why **the** sky is blue?
4. That is **a** Caribbean island.

5. **The** Hanging Gardens of Babylon were famous throughout the ancient world.
6. Is this your first time in Uris Hall?
7. **The** Natural History Museum is located on West 81st Street.
8. No pedestrians are allowed to cross **the** Queensboro Bridge.
9. Koreans share a border with **the** Chinese.
10. **The** New York Presbyterian Hospital has a good reputation.
11. Our galaxy is one of many in **the** universe.
12. Wombat Canyon is a dangerous place to go.
13. Who wouldn't like to sail to **the** Caribbean?
14. **The** Hotel California is mentioned in a well-known song.
15. One of the most scenic rivers in this area is **the** Hudson.
16. The conference will be held at **the** Westin.
17. **The** Nile is one of the longest rivers on earth.
18. Tonga is an island located in **the** Pacific Ocean.
19. Henry Ford founded **the** Ford Motor Company.
20. **The** Japanese are famous for their food.
21. One place to go shopping is Manhattan Mall, which is located on Sixth Avenue and 32nd Street.
22. General Motors is a competitor of **the** Ford Motor Company.
23. **The** Sahara Desert is located in Africa.
24. The Sheridan is a boat that travels **the** Atlantic.
25. Mr. Jones was the pilot of **a** Missouri River steamboat.
26. I am not sure if I prefer Shea Stadium as it is now or **the** old Shea Stadium.
27. **The** Bronx Zoo has so many different kinds of mammals.
28. Have you ever been to Lake Superior or Mt. Everest?

9.6 Few vs. a Few & Little vs. a Little

What is the difference in meaning in these sentences?

I have *a few* friends.	This sentence has a positive meaning: I have some friends.
I have *few* friends.	This sentence has a negative meaning: I do not have many friends.
I have *a little* energy.	This sentence has a positive meaning: I have some energy.
I have *little* energy.	This sentence has a negative meaning: I do not have much energy.

Sample Sentences:
Use nouns such as *money, time, friend, experience, memory, gas, change, sympathy, information, pollution, people, kid, class, idea* to complete the sentences below. **For each sentence, use either *a few/a little* or *few/little*.**
1. I had a hard childhood so **I have few childhood friends.**
2. I'm so broke! **I have little money since my big trip last month.**
3. Only after I turned on the engine did I realize that the car **had little gas left.**
4. After she failed out of college, her parents **had little sympathy for her.**
5. She is never lonely because she **has a few friends who live in her neighborhood so she can see them whenever she wants.**
6. Whenever I think about traveling to a new place, I realize that I **have little experience traveling!**
7. Whenever I think about writing my dissertation, I feel so nervous because **I know little about the topic, even now.**

Sample Sentences:

1. water

a. **There is little water left in the reservoir in town due to the drought this summer.**

b. **I have a little water in my bag. Do you want some?**

2. languages

a. **Few languages are as hard as Mandarin Chinese because of its four tones.**

b. **Thanks to the rigorous program in my high school, I have already studied a few languages in depth.**

Chapter 8

Grammar Specifics - Use of Prepositions

8.1 Until, By, Since, During

What's the difference between "by" and "until"?
Pay your bills *by* the end of the month.
I'm usually asleep *by* 12.
I have to hand in my essay *by* Friday.
The letter should get there *by* next week.

She waited *until* the intermission before she left.
They studied *until* 2 in the morning.
The trains in London run *until* midnight.

What's the meaning of "until" with a negative verb?
The store doesn't open *until* 10.
Don't wait *until* next week to pay your bills!

What's the meaning of "during"?
During the game, I was so bored!
I stepped out for a minute *during* the break.
What are you going to do *during* your summer vacation?

What's the meaning of "since"?
What verb tense is used with "since"?
I've worked for Chase *since* last year.
Since childhood I've been interested in classical music.
I've been playing the piano *since* 1990.

Complete the following sentences with your own ideas.
1. (by/until)
Study this sentence_____
2. (during/since)
I haven't seen him _____
3. (by/until)

Make sure you're home_____

4. (during/since)

I always go fishing_____

5. If you don't finish your homework _____

6. The store doesn't usually open_____

Fill in the blanks with *during, since, until,* or *by*.

The two brothers had not been back to their grandparents' house _____ 1992. They had been working in foreign countries _____ their college days. Both of their grandparents had died _____ the past year, and now Bob and Bud had come to get the house ready to sell. They promised to meet up _____ noon on Friday, but the weather was terrible so they didn't arrive _____ almost 6:00 p.m. It had been raining in torrents _____ their arrival and _____ their travels they had both been a little worried.

"I haven't seen such weather _____ the hurricane that blew across Mexico last year. Some good will come of it, though. They say it hasn't rained in this area _____ May," Bob said.

Their dog was nervous and restless _____ the worst part of the storm, especially when the electricity went off.

"Don't worry," Bud said to the dog. "Wait _____ later and I'll get you something good to eat."

Just then it began to hail. It hailed _____ bedtime. Bob read by candlelight _____ almost midnight. His brother listened to the radio _____ the end of the program. The dog waited patiently for his treat _____ finally giving up and going to sleep.

Sometime _____ the night the roof began to leak. _____ morning, there were puddles everywhere. They mopped up puddles _____the early evening. Unfortunately, the telephone didn't work _____ nightfall.

8.2 At

Places in the Neighborhood & Places in Your House
at +
the library
the salon
the bakery
the garage
the hospital
school
the shop
the red light
the market
12th Street
the airport
church

at +
the desk
the table
the gate
the window
the door
the computer

Describing the Exact Position in Relation to Something Bigger
at +
the end of the
the back of the
the side of the
the front of the
the bottom of the
the top of the
the corner of the
the edge of the

Attending Meetings, Appointments, Obligations, Institutions
at +
work
the meeting
lunch
university
the dentist
soccer practice

Describing the State or Manner of Something: Adjective or Adverb Phrase
at peace, at attention, at risk, at rest, at ease

Verbs with "at": Movement, Special Attention, or Facial Expression

| stare at | glare at | laugh at | look at | yell at | claw at |
| shoot at | throw at | aim at | swing at | growl at | snap at |

Emotional Reactions & Responses: Verbs & Adjectives

verbs:

cheer at   clap at   rejoice at   stand up at   cry at   celebrate at

adjectives:

astounded at   shocked at   nervous at   indignant at   upset at

surprised at   speechless at   astonished at   thrilled at   amazed at   horrified at

Describing Skills, Talents & Abilities: Nouns & Adjectives

adjectives:

good at , great at, super at, bad at, terrible at, skilled at, talented at

nouns:

a whiz at, an expert at, a pro at, a star at, an amateur at, an old hand at

Time

at 3:30, at midnight, at sunrise, at the beginning, at first, at halftime, at dawn, at dusk

at bedtime, at the same time, at different times, at one time, at once, at the end, at noon

Numbers: age, level, cost, speed, rate, degree, level

at his age   at the speed limit   at 1,000 feet   at a 25% discount   at 8mph

at age 21   at 33 degrees   at level one   at top speed   at full price

Review of "at"

Insert "at" in the paragraph in the appropriate places.

The party was scheduled to start 9 p.m. on Saturday night her friend's apartment 511 West 80th Street on Halloween night two years ago. Katie was a sophomore Economics major Blackfield University and she had been looking forward to this party for a long time. The reason was because she knew that her crush would be the party, and she was hoping to see him and get to know him a little better. (5)

She arrived her friend's apartment early with some drinks, parked her car in the parking lot the side of the building, and rang the doorbell. Her friend came to the door once. When she opened the door, Katie was shocked her friend Carly's Halloween costume – she was dressed as a pumpkin, all in orange! Carly proudly showed off her bright orange pumpkin costume and looked Katie carefully to check out her friend's outfit. Carly was impressed Katie's costume, and asked her where she bought it. Katie proudly smiled, and reminded Carly that she was fairly talented sewing, so she had made it herself. Carly smiled her, and then admitted that the pumpkin costume had been on sale the bargain store, where she bought it a discount of 40% off. While Katie excelled sewing and fashion design, Carly was pretty good shopping. (12)

As Katie helped Carly to get the apartment ready for the guests, who were supposed to arrive 8 or 9, she noticed that Carly seemed a little nervous the idea of having so many new people in her apartment. So Katie decided to make some cocktails for both of them, because she thought this would make her friend feel ease. (3)

Unfortunately, Katie drank too many of her own cocktails. First she was excited and energetic, and yelled people as they came in or waved them when she greeted them the door. A little while later, however, Katie started to feel dizzy and tired. Her "crush," who she had met a volunteer committee meeting, arrived, but she was too ill to speak to him. Finally, she had to go to bed, even though the party wasn't over yet. (4)

The next morning, sitting her computer to write an email to Carly, Katie felt really disappointed her behavior. She wished she hadn't had so many cocktails! (2)

8.3 By

Proximity – "Beside/Near"
 by the window, by the door, by the teacher, by the lake, by the post office, by the microphone, by the taxi stand

The Way Something Is Done: Certain/Special Means
 by check   by fax   by bus   by plane   by taxi
 by writing   by cutting   by swimming   by listening   by working hard

Expressing the "Agent" in a Passive Voice Sentence
 Buildings are usually designed by architects.
 The play was written by Shakespeare.
 The books have been stolen by one of the students.

Time: Not Later Than, Before a Certain Time
 by Wednesday, by the earliest possible date, by the deadline, by next Monday, by the end of the week

Move Past, Beyond, or Up To: Verbs
 walk by   sail by   march by   file by   go by   pass by
 fall by   roll by   fly by   drive by   come by   stroll by

Origin, Source, & Occupation
 by nature, by birth, by disposition, by profession, by reputation, by accident

Alone or Without Help
 by + oneself: by myself, by herself, by ourselves, by themselves, by himself

Review of "At" & "By"

Fill in the blanks with either "at" or "by".

1 Nancy lives _____ 610 South Walter Reade Avenue.

2 The Baders live _____ the new IMAX Theater, which is a great location.

3 Our plane arrived _____ 3:00 p.m.

4 Please try to be here _____ nine o'clock, as we have to check your papers and then leave promptly _____ 9:15 in order to get there on time.

5 The letter should be _____ the post office _____ now.

6 Don't sit near the bookcase! Sit _____ the window so that you can feel the cool breeze.

7 You'd better sit _____ the desk, not the coffee table, if you want to study effectively.

8 We keep the canned tuna and beans _____ the other tins.

9 Jamie is _____ the barber shop, which is _____ the pharmacy.

10 Dan improved his reading scores _____ studying hard.

11 Little kids are really quick _____ learning foreign languages.

12 The baby smiled _____ the clown who was sitting _____ himself.

13 Have you ever seen a film _____ that new director who was _____ the premier last night?

14 Would you rather arrive _____ your wedding _____ limo or _____ helicopter?

8.4 Of

Belonging, Possession, Connection
the name of   the pages of   the memories of   the hands of   the wheels of
the banks of   the scenes of   the cycles of   the pieces of   the title of

Describing Senses and Sizes: Smell, Taste, Texture, Shape, Size, Sound
the smell of   the size of   the width of   the sound of
the taste of   the feel of   the aroma of   the whistle of
the texture of   the sight of   the flavor of   the cry of

Describing Position with Direction & Place Words
the front of the house   the back of the bus
the end of the block   the side of the building
the middle of the road   the back of the drawer

Material: Be made of
made of steel   made of silk   made of cotton   made of plastic

Containers & Sets
containers: a box of, a carton of, a book of, a packet of, a can of, a tin of, a tube of
sets: a series of, a book of, a collection of, a set of, a sequence of

Measuring Parts of a Whole: Quantities, Sums, Fractions, Groups
a slice of bread, all of us, a piece of pie, a teaspoon of sugar, a pinch of salt, half of them

Position, Title, Occupation, or Role
head of   president of   leader of   secretary of
manager of   town of   master of   doctor of

Origin & Membership
people of, animals of, Indians of, countries of, graduates of, citizens of, members of

Literary, Artistic & Musical Works
works of Shakespeare   films of that director   the symphonies of Beethoven

Recorded Works & Documents
an account of   a record of   a register of   a painting of   a photograph of

Expressing Separation: Verbs, Nouns, Adjectives
verbs: get rid of   be free of   rob of   relieve of   free of
nouns: a loss of   a release of   a freedom of   a removal of
adjectives: deprived of   relieved of   cured of   free of   independent of

Expressing Reactions & Actions: "Full of Emotion"
words of anger   tears of rage   a gasp of shock   shouts of delight
a smile of chagrin   a sigh of relief   a look of horror   a tear of joy

Connecting Causes & Results
fear of flying   stress of worry   anxiety of taking a test   love of swimming

Possessing or Containing
a land of beauty   a man of honor   the ring of truth   a writer of genius
people of power   a vow of silence   a place of peace   a creature of habit

Filled with or used for a Special Purpose
a time of rest   a day of remembrance   a moment of silence
an hour of reading   a place of relaxation   a period of mourning

Dates & Times

the 15th of April   the first day of the month   ten minutes of three
the start of June   the end of the year   the 4th of July

Emotions & Their Objects
fond of   afraid of   capable of   tired of   suspicious of
envious of   bored of   aware of   ashamed of   proud of

Verbs with "of"
approve of   smell of   despair of   repent of   beware of
dream of   disapprove of   think of   reek of   stink of

Describing People's Actions: Adjectives
nice of   silly of   selfish of   kind of   cruel of   rude of

Review of "of"

Insert "of" into the paragraph below.

On the 30th October my twentieth year, my trip to China turned from hopes and dreams into real life. From childhood, I had cherished tales exploration and in particular I had been fascinated with the countries and peoples Asia.

For years, my parents disapproved this dream, thinking it was ridiculous me to think such an expensive and time-consuming trip. However, in a city there is never a lack jobs so I easily worked part the time as a math tutor, and also in the library the school of arts and sciences.

After years planning, the day departure came at last. I was afraid being late for my flight so I arrived at the airport three hours early. My bags were full maps and travel guides and I couldn't help letting out a short exhalation excitement from time to time. I was planning to use my digital camera to take lots of photographs these lands mystery, and I had packed a whole case film so that I would have enough.

The first stop my trip was Shanghai. The memory that day is one the most special my whole life. I sat at the front of the plane and gazed at the buildings below as we landed. It was the end a long flight and the start a wonderful new episode.

8.5   For

Help, Benefit, Positive Usage: Direction Something Is Sent Or Given, Reason Something Is Used
I make cookies for my kids.
Bobby had to write a story for school.
The phone call is for you.

Special Purpose
The desk is for studying.
This path is for cycling.

Substitution: Thing for Thing & Person for Person
things: I am using this box for a chair.
               I sometimes use this coffee table for a desk.
people: Sara does homework for me.
               The lawyer's assistant responds to email for him.

Showing Favor, Support, Defense, Preservation: Verbs & Nouns
verbs: vote for, fight for, run for, work for, cheer for, root for, pray for, campaign for
nouns: respect for, love for, speech for, work for, exchange for, effort for

Direction of Movement Towards a Destination: Verbs
sail for   leave for   depart for   head for   run for   sail for

Intangible Purpose or Goal
for relaxation   for amusement   for fun   for inspiration
for kicks   for entertainment   for the sake of it   for peace of mind

Desire & Longing: Verbs & Adjectives
verbs: beg for, starve for, plead for, cry for, long for, yearn for, wish for, hope for
adjectives: eager for, greedy for, anxious for, ambitious for, hungry for, thirsty for

Explaining the Meaning
Green is for go.
Red is for stop.
Sci-fi stands for "science fiction."
The Italian word for food is "cibo."

Payment, Price & Amount
The apples are two for a dollar.
You can watch a movie for almost nothing on the internet.
The elderly travel for lower fares.
I got this new hat for a great price.

Causes & Effects
causes: congratulate for, apologize for, scold for, punish for, reward for
results: famous for, good for, necessary for, important for, bad for, helpful for

Time: Duration & Appointed Time
duration: for 3 hours, for 10 miles, for 2 minutes, for a while, for a bit, for months,
for the summer,for the night, for a week, for now, for ages, for a second, for a moment
appointed time: for Thanksgiving, for tomorrow, for tonight, for the year, for the winter

Review of "for"
Insert "for" in the sentences below.
1. I have been studying 3 weeks this test because it is really important our final grade in this class. (3)
2. I am running errands my mom today because she's leaving Greece tomorrow and she's really excited her vacation. Since I'm staying with her the month, I don't really mind doing a small favor her. (5)
3. Inspiration, I sometimes visit the Buddhist temple which is located in the mountains and I stay a few days. Whenever I am desperate some peace of mind, I head the hills and it's usually so beneficial my mental, physical, and spiritual health. (5)
4. Children can attend this event a low price because the whole thing was organized charity anyway. (2)

8.6 On

Touching or Connected to
the tires on the bike   the name on the invitation   the dog on the rug
sit on the sofa   sign on the dotted line   wear a ring on your finger
Movement Toward, Touching or Reaching
throw a pillow on the bed   pour milk on the cereal   shine light on his face
Movement Against or Opposing
pound on the roof   march on the White House   make a raid on the cookie jar
Position: Next to or At the Edge of
the house on the beach   seats on the baseline   a line on both sides of the street
Position: Direction or Nearness
on my left   on the right   on the far side   on the north side
Using or Through the Use of
watch the news on TV   live on fast food   travel on a budget
buy a new house on credit   arrive on foot   chat on the phone
Regarding a Topic
a speech on   a report on   a discussion on   a seminar on   a paper on
thoughts on   comments on   ideas on   news on   vote on
Condition, State & Status
on hold   on vacation   on course   on fire   on their best behavior
Membership & Participation
on the committee   on the team   on the faculty   on the board   on the squad
Following & Resulting from
On hearing the news, he left immediately.
I got the book on request.
On second thought, he realized I was correct.
We made the decision for you on the assumption that you wouldn't mind.
Method of Travel (except for cars, trucks, RV's, small boats)
on a cruise   on a ship   on a yacht   on a sled   on a plane   on foot
on a bike   on a train   on a tour   on a journey   on a flight   on the subway
Days, Dates, Times, & Special Days (or Days Described by an Adjective)
on my birthday   on Sunday   on the fifteenth   on May 28th   on the hour
on the first Monday   on time   on a sunny day   on weekdays   on cold days

Review of "on"
Answer the following questions by writing sentences using "on".
1 You are going on a skiing trip next week. How would you prefer to travel?
2 When was the last time you saw a full moon?
3 How do you usually get the news?
4 Where is your house located?
5 What is the reason for the protest?
6 Where do you prefer to wear jewelry?
7 Where do you have photographs hanging in your house?
8 When you go away on a trip, what is your status?
9 Are you a member of any groups, committees, or clubs?
10 What is the position of the door in relation to you right now?

8.7   In

Containment & Immersion: Physical or Abstract
in the ocean	in this area	in our imagination	in the USA
in the purse	in the refrigerator	in memory	in Chicago
in the sand	in the doorway	in the paper	in your pocket

"in" + Nouns of Emotion & Reaction
in amazement   in awe   in pain   in anger   in sorrow

State or Condition
in competition   in secret   in view   in a hurry   in love

Using
write a check in pen, draw a picture in blue, decorate in plaid, speak in French

Portrayed or Shown
The article in the paper was wrong.
The information in the records was accurate.
The character in the book was likable.

Wearing Clothes & Accessories
the man in the tall hat, the girl in black, the poor children in rags, the officers in uniform, the model in the designer clothes, the boys in shorts, the dancer in the tutu

Employment & Participation
That doctor works in medicine.
Their family has been in the theatre for generations.
I just realized that your father works in film.
The girls in the dance club are so busy.

Divided, Organized or Arranged
in piles	in bunches	in order	in lines	in groups	in a circle
in stacks	in tiers	in sections	in teams	in rows	in a block

Method of Travel: Cars, Trucks, RV's, small boats
in a car   in his RV   in the subway car   in a canoe   in a rowboat

Time: Season, Year, Month & Time of Day (except dawn, noon, night or midnight)
in summer   in 1982   in August   in the morning   in the daytime

Review of "in" and "on"
Fill in the blanks with "in" or "on."

1 His name was _____ the attendance chart and he looked just like the little boy _____ the cover of my favorite book _____ the library.

2 She always has a smile _____ her face even though she is usually _____ a hurry.

3 _____ December the students were _____ the middle of their final exam when a fire alarm interrupted us. _____ hearing the alarm, we all looked up _____ shock because we knew we would have to abandon our test _____ vectors and put it _____ hold in order to line up _____ groups by class _____ the side of the school's main entrance.

4 _____ a whim, I decided to give my opinion _____ the book during the class discussion even though I knew my classmates would wage a group assault _____ my ideas. The people _____ the class tend to have views _____ politics which are pretty different from mine.

8.8 ANSWER KEY

10.1 Until, By, Since, During

What's the difference between "by" and "until"?

"By" means *not later than, or to be completed on or **before a certain time.***

"Until" means *up to the time when, or up to as **late as.***

What's the meaning of "until" with a negative verb?

"Until" with a negative verb means ***before a certain time.***

What's the meaning of "during"?

"During" means *throughout a period of time that something else is happening.*

What's the meaning of "since"?

"Since" means *from a (specified) past time up to the present.*

What verb tense is used with "since"?

"Since" usually requires present perfect or past perfect.

Sample Sentences:

1. (by/until) Study this sentence **until you understand it.**
2. (during/since) I haven't seen him **since our lunch break.**
3. (by/until) Make sure you're home **by 10:30 tonight.**
4. (during/since) I always go fishing **during the summer vacation.**
5. If you don't finish your homework **by dinner time**, I'm not taking you to the movies.
6. The store doesn't usually open **until 8:00 in the morning.**

Correct Answers:

The two brothers had not been back to their grandparents' house **since** 1992. They had been working in foreign countries **during** their college days. Both of their grandparents had died **during** the past year, and now Bob and Bud had come to get the house ready to sell. They promised to meet up **by** noon on Friday, but the weather was terrible so they didn't arrive **until** almost 6:00 p.m. It had been raining in torrents **since** their arrival and **during** their travels they had both been a little worried.

"I haven't seen such weather **since** the hurricane that blew across Mexico last year. Some good will come of it, though. They say it hasn't rained in this area **since** May," Bob said.

Their dog was nervous and restless **during** the worst part of the storm, especially when the electricity went off.

"Don't worry," Bud said to the dog. "Wait **until** later and I'll get you something good to eat."

Just then it began to hail. It hailed **until** bedtime. Bob read by candlelight **until** almost midnight. His brother listened to the radio **until** the end of the program. The dog waited patiently for his treat **until** finally giving up and going to sleep.

Sometime **during** the night the roof began to leak. **By** morning, there were puddles everywhere. They mopped up puddles **until** the early evening. Unfortunately, the telephone didn't work **until** nightfall.

10.2 At

Correct Answers for "Review of 'at'":

The party was scheduled to start **at** 9 p.m. on Saturday night **at** her friend's apartment **at** 511 West 80th Street on Halloween night two years ago. Katie was a sophomore Economics major **at** Blackfield University and she had been looking forward to this party for a long time. The reason was because she knew that her crush would be **at** the party, and she was hoping to see him and get to know him a little better. (5)

She arrived **at** her friend's apartment early with some drinks, parked her car in the parking lot **at** the side of the building, and rang the doorbell. Her friend came to the door **at** once. When she opened the door, Katie was shocked **at** her friend Carly's Halloween costume – she was dressed as a pumpkin, all in orange! Carly proudly showed off her bright orange pumpkin costume and looked **at** Katie carefully to check out her friend's outfit. Carly was impressed **at** Katie's costume, and asked her where she bought it. Katie proudly smiled, and reminded Carly that she was fairly talented **at** sewing, so she had made it herself. Carly smiled **at** her, and then admitted that the pumpkin costume had been on sale **at** the bargain store, where she bought it **at** a discount of 40% off. While Katie excelled **at** sewing and fashion design, Carly was pretty good **at** shopping. (12)

As Katie helped Carly to get the apartment ready for the guests, who were supposed to arrive **at** 8 or 9, she noticed that Carly seemed a little nervous **at** the idea of having so many new people in her apartment. So Katie decided to make some cocktails for both of them, because she thought this would make her friend feel **at** ease. (3)

Unfortunately, Katie drank too many of her own cocktails. First she was excited and energetic, and yelled **at** people as they came in or waved **at** them when she greeted them **at** the door. A little while later, however, Katie started to feel dizzy and tired. Her "crush," who she had met **at** a volunteer committee meeting, arrived, but she was too ill to speak to him. Finally, she had to go to bed, even though the party wasn't over yet. (4)

The next morning, sitting **at** her computer to write an email to Carly, Katie felt really disappointed **at** her behavior. She wished she hadn't had so many cocktails! (2)

10.3 By

Answers to "Review of 'at' and 'by':

1. Nancy lives **at** 610 South Walter Reade Avenue.

2. The Baders live **by** the new IMAX Theater, which is a great location.

3. Our plane arrived **at** 3:00 p.m.

4. Please try to be here **by** nine o'clock, as we have to check your papers and then leave promptly **at** 9:15 in order to get there on time.

5. The letter should be **at** the post office **by** now.

6. Don't sit near the bookcase! Sit **by** the window so that you can feel the cool breeze.

7. You'd better sit **at** the desk, not the coffee table, if you want to study effectively.

8. We keep the canned tuna and beans **by** the other tins.

9. Jamie is **at** the barber shop, which is **by** the pharmacy. 10. Dan improved his reading scores **by** studying hard.

11. Little kids are really quick **at** learning foreign languages.

12. The baby smiled **at** the clown who was sitting **by** himself.

13. Have you ever seen a film **by** that new director who was **at** the premier last night?

14. Would you rather arrive **at** your wedding **by** limo or **by** helicopter?

10.4 Of

Answers to "Review of 'of'":

On the 30th **of** October **of** my twentieth year, my trip to China turned from hopes and dreams into real life. From childhood, I had cherished tales **of** exploration and in particular I had been fascinated with the countries and peoples **of** Asia.

For years, my parents disapproved **of** this dream, thinking it was ridiculous **of** me to think **of** such an expensive and time-consuming trip. However, in a city there is never a lack **of** jobs so I easily worked part **of** the time as a math tutor, and also in the library **of** the school of arts and sciences.

After years planning, the day **of** departure came at last. I was afraid **of** being late for my flight so I arrived at the airport three hours early. My bags were full **of** maps and travel guides and I couldn't help letting out a short exhalation **of** excitement from time to time. I was planning to use my digital camera to take lots **of** photographs **of** these lands of mystery, and I had packed a whole case **of** film so that I would have enough.

The first stop **of** my trip was Shanghai. The memory **of** that day is one **of** the most special **of** my whole life. I sat at the front of the plane and gazed at the buildings below as we landed. It was the end **of** a long flight and the start **of** a wonderful new episode.

10.5 For

Answers to "Review of 'for'":

1. I have been studying **for** 3 weeks this **for** test because it is really important **for** our final grade in this class. (3)

2. I am running errands **for** my mom today because she's leaving **for** Greece tomorrow and she's really excited **for** her vacation. Since I'm staying with her **for** the month, I don't really mind doing a small favor **for** her. (5)

3. **For** inspiration, I sometimes visit the Buddhist temple which is located in the mountains and I stay **for** a few days. Whenever I am desperate **for** some peace of mind, I head **for** the hills and it's usually so beneficial **for** my mental, physical, and spiritual health. (5)

4. Children can attend this event **for** a low price because the whole thing was organized **for** charity anyway. (2)

10.6 On

Sample Sentences:

1. You are going on a skiing trip next week. How would you prefer to travel? **I would prefer to travel <u>on foot even though I know it's impossible!</u>**

2. When was the last time you saw a full moon? **I saw one <u>on the fourth of July</u>** last year.

3. How do you usually get the news? **I usually watch the news <u>on TV.</u>**

4. Where is your house located? **My house is located <u>on 34th Street</u> between Lexington and Park.**

5. What is the reason for the protest? **They are protesting to express their opinion <u>on abortion.</u>**

6. Where do you prefer to wear jewelry? **I love to wear jewelry <u>on my hands and wrists.</u>**

7. Where do you have photographs hanging in your house? **There are some pictures <u>on my walls and on my refrigerator.</u>**

8. When you go away on a trip, what is your status? **At that point, I am <u>on vacation!</u>**

9. Are you a member of any groups, committees, or clubs? **I am <u>on the PTA holiday committee this year.</u>**

10. What is the position of the door in relation to you right now? **The door to this room is <u>on my left.</u>**

10.7 In

Answers to "Review of 'in' and 'on'":

1. His name was **on** the attendance chart and he looked just like the little boy **on** the cover of my favorite book **in** the library.

2. She always has a smile **on** her face even though she is usually **in** a hurry.

3. **In** December the students were **in** the middle of their final exam when a fire alarm interrupted us. **On** hearing the alarm, we all looked up **in** shock because we knew we would have to abandon our test **on** vectors and put it **on** hold in order to line up **in** groups by class **on** the side of the school's main entrance.

4. **On** a whim, I decided to give my opinion **on** the book during the class discussion even though I knew my classmates would wage a group assault **on** my ideas. The people **in** the class tend to have views **on** politics which are pretty different from mine.

Chapter 9

Presentational Skills

Speaking before a group requires practice. Even the most outgoing or experienced individuals need to prepare for making presentations in front of audiences. First, we will offer some suggestions for preparing the content of your presentation. Then we will discuss perfecting your delivery and engaging your audience. Finally, we will focus on speaking in different kinds of situations.

9.1 Prepare the Content

Before speaking in front of a group, draft the content of your presentation. Give yourself enough time in advance to prepare.

Define Your Goal & Agenda

First, define your goal. The goal of your presentation is the total effect you want to achieve. It should be clear and specific. Try to reduce the goal of your entire presentation to a sentence of no more than 10 words. **Do you want to inform, entertain, persuade, or consult?**

Next, begin writing your presentation and state your agenda. The agenda you want to follow should result directly from your goal.

- **Set an agenda**

  - Compose three or four key points that can be stated in one or two sentences.

  - These are the key points you would like your audience to remember.

  - Use the agenda throughout the presentation.

Keep Your Audience in Mind

Tailoring your presentation towards your audience's needs and interests may be the most effective way to achieving your goal. Think about who they are and how you can appeal to them.

- **Know the expectation and the setting**

  - Who is the audience? What is their cultural or corporate background? How diverse is the group? What is their knowledge level of the subject matter?

  - How many times have they heard similar presentations? What is their expectation level? How can you appeal to them?

- Are there any key decision-makers? How do you make your delivery unique and memorable?
- Will your presentation be live or taped?
- Will you be the focus or are you to be included in a larger forum?

Ways to Open

The opening of your presentation is crucial. You need to captivate the audience within a few minutes. Keep the closing of your presentation in mind as you design the opening so that you may ensure coherency and reinforcement of the central message.

- Useful openings

  - Tell a short, interesting, and related story or joke
  - Ask the audience to do something
  - Preview your agenda
  - Introduce yourself and state your goal and its relevance to your audience
  - Ask a question
  - Make an unexpected strong statement
  - Quote an impressive statistic

Structure the Body

The body of your presentation needs to be focused on your precise purpose in order to maintain the attention of your audience. You must continually bring your audience's attention back to your subject throughout the delivery process.

- When constructing presentation slides, you should

  - Use no more than 4 to 5 lines of text per page.
  - Use color, boldface or large-size type fonts for emphasis and variety.
  - Organize your presentation in a clear logic or timeline.
  - Highlight key takeaway points from each slide and throughout the entire presentation. Make your writing an effective communication medium rather than a tool to organize your own thoughts.

Write the Closing

Because it is the last thing the audience hears, the closing will most likely be remembered. The close should include a clear and powerful statement of your message.
Think about the closing before designing the opening. That way your entire presentation will more likely reinforce your primary message through a common thread with repeated useful facts and/or opinions.

- There are a few common ways to end a presentation:

  - A recap
  - A call for action or a recommendation
  - A Q&A session

9.2 Perfect Delivery & Engaging Your Audience

After you know what you will discuss, focus on how you will deliver your message. There are three building blocks of communication when you are making a presentation in front of an audience:

(1) Verbal

(2) Non-verbal

(3) Audio-Visual

9.2.1 Verbal

To engage your audience, be aware of vocal variations. **You have the power not only to influence your audience with what you say, but how you say it.** There are four primary elements of the voice to consider: pitch, volume, pace and articulation.

(1) **Pitch** refers to how high or low a tone is. Add variation and inflection in your pitch to avoid monotony. You do not want to sound like you are bored.

(2) Finding the perfect **volume** is also important. Speak loudly enough to be heard by the people seated in the rear of the room.

(3) Also, use a **pace** that is easy to follow and allows the listener to hear all the words clearly. Know when to take a pause to give the listener time to process information. Pauses also add needed variety to your speech.

(4) Finally, **articulation** refers to how clearly sounds are enunciated. Speak clearly and pronounce every syllable without overdoing it or appearing unnatural. **Do not mumble and drop off at the end of a sentence.**

Most importantly, keep a good balance by varying all four vocal elements. It will help you make your points and your listeners improve their comprehension.

9.2.2 Non-verbal

The non-verbal aspects of communication, which are important when making a presentation, include **dress, stance, movement, gesturing and eye contact.**
Your audience's first impression of you will be based on how your present yourself. Needless to say, first impressions are critical, just like your opening remarks. **Enhance your credibility by looking professional and reliable.** Wear something that will help you feel confident and comfortable.
In addition, you need to **walk with assurance** in front of the room. Plant your feet apart and stand firmly. Pull you shoulders back. Remember to hold you head straight as well.
If the layout of the room permits, you should **use movement** to draw attention to a visual aid, move closer or away from the audience, make a pause, facilitate a transition, or reinforce a message. However, do not overdo it. Pacing, rocking and swaying can be distracting and annoying and may indicate nervousness.

Use gestures to emphasize your message. Whether or not you should use small hand and arm movements or bigger ones depends on the size of the room. For example, in a tiered lecture classroom holding 200 people, broader movements are more visible to the audience. Avoid nervous gestures that distract attention.

Effective eye contact is perhaps the most important aspect of non-verbal communication during your presentation. Look at your audience while you talk. You will appear more confident and your presentation will be more personal, persuasive and impressive. It also allows you to get a good gauge of their reaction. You can adjust your presentation accordingly.

When you present in front of a small group, meet the eyes of everyone throughout the presentation to establish a good rapport. Look at one person at a time to complete a thought or phrase. Then move on to another person without rushing. If you present in front of a large group, work the room section by section. It is important not to favor one side or the other. You can look around across the group in a Z pattern and then focus on one section at a time.

Body language, facial expression, physical presence, vocal energy and inflection all amount to the impression you make.

9.2.3 Audio-visual

Your presentation will look more prepared, professional, and dynamic if it incorporates visual aids. Visual and audio aids help the audience grasp information and can clarify complex data. Effective visual aids will support what you are saying, rather than distract or detract from the rest of your presentation.

Visual aids should be clear and organized with appropriate titles. Use phrases, not sentences. Use fonts in large, legible type.

- Tips on using visual aids

    - Check the room and equipment ahead of time
    - Make sure your visual aids are visible
    - Do not overload your audience with visual aids
    - Keep to one idea per page
    - Talk to the audience, not your visual aids
    - Write on your visual aid for interest and excitement

9.2.4 Additional Reminders

- **Organize the points you want to make.**

    - Use index cards
    - Be yourself
    - Relax

- **Test everything.**

○ Arrive early to handle any last minute unexpected situations. Know where the light switches are. Test projectors and microphones.

- **Always use simple sentences.**

  ○ Summarize a complicated answer in a few short sentences.

  ○ Avoid using fillers such as "you know".

- **Show enthusiasm.**

  ○ Captivate the audience's attention by displaying your interest in the topic

9.3 Different Situations

Question and Answer

For a Question and Answer session, be thoroughly prepared. Anticipate all the possible questions the audience may ask. Practice with a friend or colleague just like for an interview.

○ Be aware of available time for each question. If the session is well timed, make ground rules for how to raise questions and how many follow-up questions each member has. Make these rules known to the audience in the beginning. Remember to take questions from all sections of the audience.

○ You may need to rephrase the question if some audience members cannot hear clearly or the question is vague, broad or hard to understand.

○ If the question is not long-winded, focus all your attention on the questioner until she or he has finished speaking. Then shift your eye contact to others in the group. Speak to the entire group. Keep everyone interested.

○ When asked similar questions, try to summarize them or expand on prior answers and move on.

○ When asked a difficult or hostile question, always stay calm and in control. You can avoid answering some of those questions by briefly addressing them and then recommending more private discussions after the event. If you don't have an answer to a question, just say that you'll follow up promptly.

○ When asked a great question, do not hesitate to offer compliments.

When you end the session, have the final word. Do not end it with a question or remark from someone else. Call for action, make a recommendation or simply thank everyone.

Team Presentations

When preparing for a team presentation, each member should participate.

○ Meet to define goals, agenda, structure, and allocation of speaking responsibilities.

○ Rehearse as a group to make sure everyone's parts flow together. Provide clear transitions between speakers.

○ Be attentive when a group member is speaking on stage. Take notes so that the next member can adjust the delivery if necessary.

Moderating Panels

A moderator can play a different role depending on the interplay between the speakers and the moderator. Typically a moderator guides, stimulates, and controls the presentation. Be careful not to project your opinions too often. Aim for an active panel discussion while facilitating interaction between the audience and panelists.

Arrive early to make sure all the name tents are ready and in the event certain panelists arrive late or miss the event, you should adjust seats promptly. At the beginning of the panel, give a very brief introduction of yourself, the subject, the panelists and the format of the event such as the agenda, how questions will be handled, expected ending time, and any other important details.

Stay in charge of taking questions and directing them to various panelists. Control timing. At the end, summarize the main points, introduce the next event if applicable, and end on a positive note.

9.4   Summary of Tips

○ Be prepared. Carefully define the message you want to convey, collect the necessary information, and anticipate questions from the audience

○ Rehearse multiple times. Practice your delivery out loud.

○ To be a good presenter, you need to be engaging with the audience and know your topic. Use simple sentences.

○ Use an electronic enhancement, such as PowerPoint, as an accompaniment to your presentation to reinforce your point, not as a crutch.

○ Talk to the members of your audience rather than read to them.

○ Keep the presentation concise and include only relevant information.

○ Repeat essential information or take-away points.

○ YOU are the presentation, so carefully consider your movements, speech, and dress. Show your enthusiasm!

9.5 Individual Exercise

1. What are the two most important skills for business success?

2. Why did you decide to pursue xxx (for example, your major, degree or career choice)?

3. Describe a challenge that you have overcome.

4. Describe an experience that taught you a lesson about trust.

5. If you could change one thing about your home country, what would it be?

6. If you could change one thing about the United States, what would it be?

7. What new technology has significantly changed the way you live or work?

8. What do you think are more important – communication skills or analytic skills?

9. What movie or book has made a significant impression on you?

10. If you had the opportunity to live in the year 1908, 2008, or 2108, which would you choose?

11. What achievement are you most proud of?

12. Why do you think people are often afraid to risk failure?

13. If you had not pursued a career in xxx (such as business), what would you be doing now?

14. Who is an example to you of a courageous person?

15. Who is an example to you of a successful person?

16. What do you think is the most effective way to motivate someone?

17. Describe a memorable trip that you have taken.

18. If you had a choice between a vacation spent in a major city and one spent at a beach resort, which would you choose?

19. What about your time in the city of xxx (such as New York)? So far what have you found most surprising?

Chapter 10

Accent Reduction

10.1 Speech Mechanism

To articulate sounds, we use the vocal tract with the air stream generated from the lungs:

- Oral Cavity - Essentially the mouth

    - Tongue & Lips - Articulate sounds
    - Teeth - Provide acoustic partition
    - Vocal Cords - Provide sounds through vibration, which is created by muscles tightening or expanding the cords, narrowing or expanding the space between them

- Nasal Cavity - Inside the nose

- Pharyngeal Cavity - In the throat

You can hear the following elements of spoken English:

- Consonant

    - Made with a stopped or interrupted breath
    - Either through the mouth or the nose
    - Either voiced sound (with vibration through the vocal cords) or unvoiced (no vibration)

- Vowel

    - Made with a continuous airflow
    - Through the mouth only
    - Always voiced sound (with vibration through the vocal cords)

- Diphthong

    - A combination of two vowel sounds into one phonetic unit

Besides sounds, the spoken English language is also characterized by rhythm, pace, pauses, pitch, intonation and inflection.

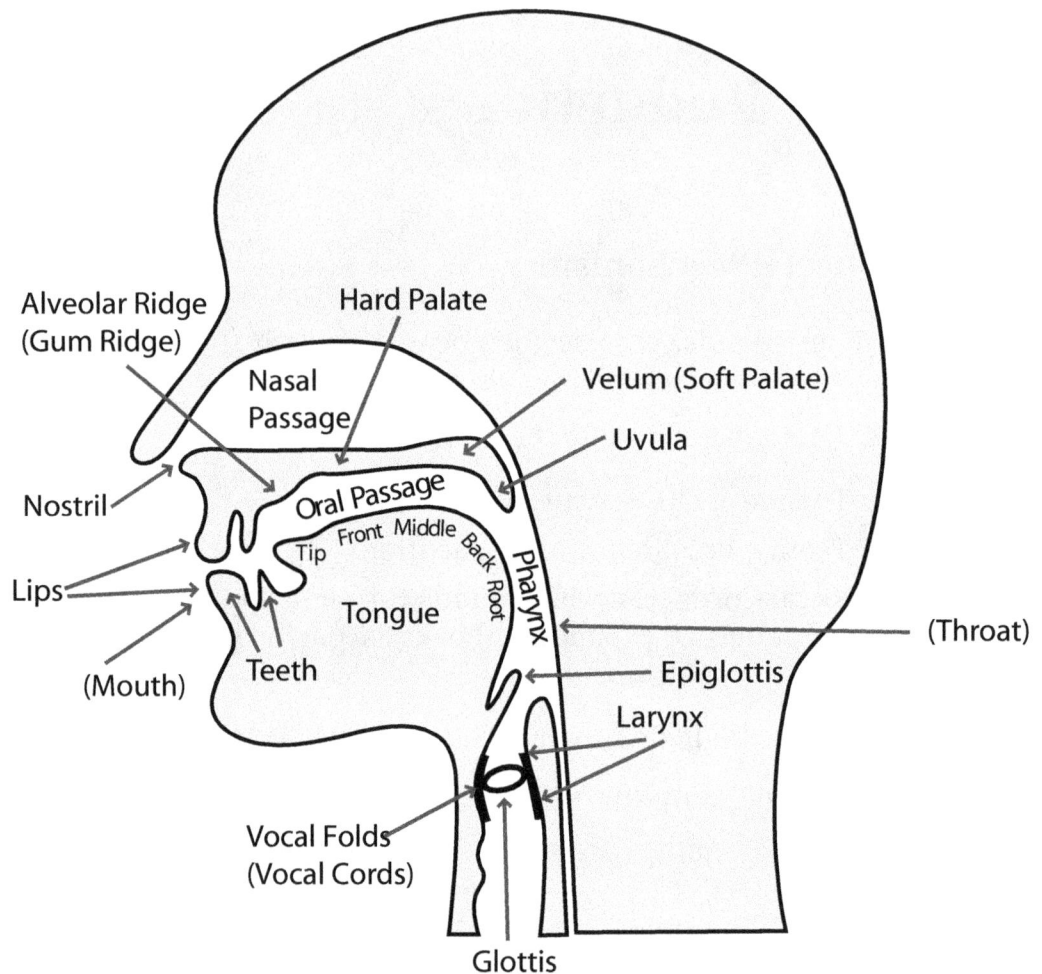

Alveolar Ridge (Gum Ridge) • **Hard Palate** • **Nasal Passage** • **Velum (Soft Palate)** • **Uvula** • **Nostril** • **Oral Passage** • **Tip** **Front** **Middle** **Back** **Root** • **Pharynx** • **Lips** • **Tongue** • **(Throat)** • **(Mouth)** • **Teeth** • **Epiglottis** • **Larynx** • **Vocal Folds (Vocal Cords)** • **Glottis**

10.2   Consonants

Nasal Consonants "m," "n," "ng"
For all three sounds, the soft palate is relaxed and lowered. The vibrated breath will move through the nasal passage, not through the mouth.
For the "m" sound (as in _me, thumb_ and _condemn_):
- The lower jaw and tongue are relaxed.
- The lips are touching and closed.
- The vibrated air goes out through the nose.

For the "n" sound (as in _not, gnu_ and _pneumonic_):
- The lower jaw and tongue are relaxed.
- The mouth is half open, so the top and bottom lips do not touch.
- The tip of the tongue is raised. `
- The tip of the tongue touches the gum ridge, directly behind the upper front teeth.
- The vibrated air goes out through the nose.

For the "ng" sound (as in _bring_):
- The lower jaw and tongue are relaxed.
- The mouth is half open, so the top and bottom lips do not touch.
- The back of the tongue is raised.
- The back of the tongue touches the soft palate.
- The vibrated air goes out through the nose.

Plosive Consonants "p," "b," "t," "d," "k," and "g"

For the "p" sound (as in _pop_):
- The lips are tightly shut.
- The vocal chords do not vibrate, so voiceless air is exhaled in an explosion of pressure.
- The lips are opened quickly, and the air comes out in a small pop or puff.

For the "b" sound (as in _ripe_ and _cupboard_):
- This sound is the voiced counterpart of the "p" sound.
- The lips are tightly shut.
- The vocal chords vibrate, so voiced or buzzed air is exhaled in an explosion of pressure.
- The lips are opened quickly, and the air comes out in a small pop or puff.

For the "t" sound (as in _rat, thought, slapped_, and _receipt_)
- The tip of the tongue is taps up against the gum ridge right behind the upper teeth to block air from coming out of the mouth and then moves back down.
- The vocal chords do not vibrate, so voiced air is exhaled in a sharp puff.

For the "d" sound (as in _due_ and _bowed_):
- This sound is the voiced counterpart of the "t" sound.
- The tip of the tongue is taps up against the gum ridge right behind the upper teeth to block air from coming out of the mouth and then moves back down.
- The vocal chords do not vibrate, so voiced air is exhaled in a sharp puff.

For the "k" sound (as in _cat, chord, kit, opaque_ and _tick_):
- The back of the tongue touches the soft palate at the back of the mouth, blocking air from entering the mouth.
- The vocal chords do not vibrate.
- The tongue drops from the soft palate quickly and voiceless air comes out of the mouth in a puff.

For the "g" sound (as in _gut, ghoul, rogue_):
- This sound is the voiced counterpart of the "k" sound.
- The back of the tongue touches the soft palate at the back of the mouth, blocking air from entering the mouth.
- The vocal chords vibrate.
- The tongue drops from the soft palate quickly and voiced air comes out of the mouth in a lightly buzzed puff.

Fricative Consonants "f," "v," "s," "z," "sh," "dZ," "th," "th," and "h"

These sounds are all formed by restricting the air coming out of the mouth, forcing it into a narrow stream.

For the "f" sound (as in _full, laugh, stuff,_ and _phone_):
- The jaw is relaxed.
- The teeth rest on the bottom lip.
- The vocal chords do not vibrate.
- The voiceless air moves out of the mouth between the teeth and lower lip.

For the "v" sound (as in _voice, of,_ and _Stephen_):
- This sound is the voiced counterpart of the "f" sound.
- The jaw is relaxed.
- The teeth rest on the bottom lip.
- The vocal chords vibrate.
- The voiced, buzzed air moves out of the mouth between the teeth and lower lip

For the "s" (as in _sue_):
- The top and bottom teeth are close together, almost touching.
- The tip of the tongue is behind the teeth and is pointing up toward the gum ridge.
- The lips are spread out slightly.
- Air moves quickly down the center of the tongue toward the teeth.
- The sound is voiceless, short and sharp.

For the "z" (as in _zoo_):
- This sound is the voiced counterpart of the "s" sound.
- The top and bottom teeth are close together, almost touching.
- The tip of the tongue is behind the teeth and is pointing up toward the gum ridge.
- The lips are spread out slightly.
- The vocal chords vibrate. - The voiced air moves quickly down the center of the tongue toward the teeth.
- There is a buzzed sound and feeling in the mouth.

For the "sh" sound (as in _shot, passion, mention, issue, glacial,_ and _chauvinist_):
- The mouth is mostly closed and the lips are pushed forward and rounded, making a small "o" shape.
- The sides of the tongue make contact with the inside of the back teeth.
- The blade of the tongue touches the front part of the palate directly behind the gum ridge.
- The vocal chords do not vibrate.
- The voiceless air comes out through the narrow space between the tongue and the front of the palate.

For the "dz" sound (as in _rouge, pleasure,_ and _fusion_):
- This sound is the voiced counterpart of the "sh" sound.
- The mouth is mostly closed and the lips are pushed forward and rounded, making a small "o" shape.
- The sides of the tongue make contact with the inside of the back teeth.
- The blade of the tongue touches the front part of the palate directly behind the gum ridge.
- The vocal chords vibrate.
- The voiced air comes out through the narrow space between the tongue and the

front of the palate.

For the "th" sound (as in *thin* and *mouth*):
- The lower jaw is relaxed.
- The tip of the tongue touches the grooved edge of the top teeth.
- The soft palate is raised.
- The sides of the tongue have contact with the upper molars.
- The rim of the tongue remains broad and flat.
- The vocal chords do not vibrate.
- The voiceless air goes out between the tip of the tongue and the upper teeth in a stream.

For the "th" sound (as in *them, other,* and *mouth*):
- This sound is the voiced counterpart of the "th" sound.
- The lower jaw is relaxed.
- The tip of the tongue touches the grooved edge of the top teeth.
- The soft palate is raised.
- The sides of the tongue have contact with the upper molars.
- The rim of the tongue remains broad and flat.
- The vocal chords vibrate.
- The voiced air goes out between the tip of the tongue and the upper teeth in a stream.

For the "h" sound (as in *he, fajita,* and *whose*):
- The mouth is wide open.
- The vocal chords do not vibrate.
- Air is exhaled from the throat out of the mouth in a continuous stream.

Affricate Consonants "tf" and "dz"

These sounds use a plosive articulation, or a puff of air, as well as fricative articulation, or a restricted air flow. The exhaled air is restricted in some way using the mouth, and then the air pressure is released in a swift burst through the restricted pathway.

For the "tf" sound (as in *chat, batch, fracture* and *question*)
- The lower jaw is relaxed.
- The upper and lower teeth almost touch.
- The mouth is only slightly open.
- The front of the tongue touches the gum ridge.
- The lips are slightly pushed out.
- The front of the tongue is lowered.
- The vocal chords do not vibrate.
- An explosion of voiceless air pushes out of the mouth between the tongue and gum ridge from behind the tongue in a singular puff.

For the "dz" sound (as in *ledge, adjust, gym, collage,* and *jet*):
- This sound is the voiced counterpart of the "tf" sound.
- The lower jaw is relaxed.
- The upper and lower teeth almost touch.
- The mouth is only slightly open.
- The front of the tongue touches the gum ridge.
- The lips are slightly pushed out.
- The front of the tongue is lowered.
- The vocal chords vibrate.

- An explosion of voiced, buzzed air pushes out of the mouth between the tongue and gum ridge from behind the tongue in a singular puff.

Glide Consonants "w," "r," "l," "j"

These sounds are similar to vowel diphthongs because they begin with the mouth in one position but while making the sound the mouth shifts to a different position. Some of these sounds are called Ôsemivowels' because even their sound has a vowel-like quality.

For the "w" sound (as in _water, queen,_ and _one_):
- The lower jaw is relaxed.
- The tip of the tongue rests behind the lower teeth.
- The lips are rounded.
- The back of the tongue is arched.

For the "r" sound (as in _rut_):
- The jaw is relaxed.
- The mouth is partly open.
- The tongue is lifted to a spot behind the gum ridge.
- The tip of the tongue stays free, but is pointed toward the back of the upper gums.
- The tip of the tongue is curled.

For the "l" sound (as in _lot_):
- The tip of the tongue touches the gum ridge.
- The rest of the tongue is broad and flat so the air goes around the sides of the tongue.
- The tongue stays relaxed.

For the "j" sound (as in _yet, monsignor,_ and _junior_):
- The mouth is slightly open. The front of the tongue is raised up toward the palate.
- The vocal chords vibrate.
- The voiced air moves inward as the mouth repositions for the coming vowel sound.

10.3 Vowels

These sounds include simple vowel sounds as well as diphthongs, which are a special type of vowel formed through a combination of two different mouth positions put together. They are not two separate sounds, though they involve a shift in the position of the mouth during the production of the sound.

For the "i" sound (as in _heat, me, meet, people, conceive, relieve, machine, subpoena, key,_ and _quayside_):
- The jaw is only slightly open.
- The lips are pressed into a slight smile.
- The front of the tongue is raised, and pushes against the hard palate.
- The sides of the tongue touch the upper teeth.
- The sound is drawn out slightly.

For the "I" sound (as in _women, wit, business, surfeit,_ and _tricycle_):
- The jaw is only slightly open.
- The lips are pressed into a slight smile.
- The front of the tongue is raised toward the palate and relaxed.
- The tongue presses lightly against the inside of the upper teeth.

- The opening between the tongue and palate is round and open.
- The sound is shorter than the "i" sound.

For the "e" sound (as in *name, pail, gauge, bay, lingerie, break, weight, disobey*, and *risque*):
- The mouth is open halfway.
- The front of the tongue pointed up toward the palate.
- The lips are spread out slightly.
- As the sound is produced, the jaw closes a little and the front of the tongue comes closer to the palate.

For the "E" sound (as in *stationary, met, health, heifer, leopard, friends*, and *deaf*):
- The jaw is lowered a little.
- The front of the tongue is pointed up toward the palate.
- The muscles of the tongue are relaxed.
- The lips are spread out slightly.

The Vowel Sound "u" as in *would*
- The lower jaw is relaxed.
- The tip of the tongue rests behind the bottom front teeth.
- The back of the tongue is curved toward the soft palate.
- The lips are rounded narrowly.
- The sound is focused through the lips.

The Vowel Sound "o" as in *obey*
- The jaw is relaxed.
- The tip of the tongue is relaxed and rests behind the lower front teeth.
- The back of the tongue is curved.
- The lips are rounded into a perfect circle shape.

10.4 Diphthongs

The Diphthong Sound "ow" as in *now*
- The lower jaw is relaxed and opened wide.
- The tip of the tongue touches the back of the lower front teeth.
- The back of the tongue is curved into a low and flat position at first.
- Then the lower jaw and tongue curve upward to the second "u" position.
- The lips move from a relaxed position at first into a rounded position.

10.5 Intonation

10.5.1 Rising and Falling Tones

- *Use the appropriate tone to express your mood/feeling/attitude.*

There could be 5 different ways of pronouncing "Hello." What might be the implied meaning/context of each?

Hello

Hello

Hello

Hello
Hello

Really

Are you sure about that?

How are you?

No way

I have to do it tonight

What do you think I was doing?

Excuse me

10.5.2 Word and Syllable Stress

- *Change the word stress for emphasis of your meaning.*

I never start writing until the night before the deadline. (not you, not him, not my sister)
I **never** start writing until the night before the deadline. (not sometimes, not mostly)
I never **start** writing until the night before the deadline. (not finish, not continue)
I never start **writing** until the night before the deadline. (not preparing, not researching)
I never start writing until the **night** before the deadline. (not the day, not the morning)
I never start writing until the night before the **deadline**. (not any other day, not an earlier time)

I only watch 35 minutes of TV when I'm home alone.
- How would you emphasize TV, not a movie?
- How would you emphasize alone, not with other people?
- How would you emphasize you, not someone else?
- How would you emphasize watch, not listen to?
- How would you emphasize 35, not 34?
- How would you emphasize 35, not 45?

- *Change the word stress for emphasis of your meaning.*
1. He always gives homework to us.
2. My professor never lets us leave early.
3. You never come out for a drink after class!
4. Did you do the assignment this time?
5. I have to pass the exemption test this year.

10.5.3 Rhythm

- *Break longer sentences into shorter thought groups. There are no fixed rules for this, though you may use grammatical groupings, such as a prepositional phrase or an article + noun. Make sure you pause appropriately for a comma, semicolon, or period.*

Could you please copy me on the letter you're faxing to the CEO of the company?

I'd appreciate if you'd keep me in the loop on this matter, even while I'm away.

Jonathan is going to get fired if he doesn't start to pull his weight around here.

The landlord kept skirting the issue about when the payment is actually due.

We need to nail down the terms of our contract by tomorrow in order to have enough time to perform the services you need us to do.

Even though I busted my buns all week to get the project finished, I was still not given the appreciation I deserved for my work.

David isn't cut out to be an accountant; he isn't detail-oriented and he doesn't even like numbers.

After careful review of the budget, it is necessary that we cut back this year on useless expenses and get the ball rolling in the right direction.

10.5.4 Pronunciation of can/can't

- *Can is not stressed in most sentences and questions, and it is produced with a short, unclear vowel. Can is stressed if it comes at the end of a sentence or clause.*
- *Can't is always stressed. The vowel sound in "can't" is the same as in "hand."*

If you are a student attending our class, listen to your instructor and circle the correct choice.

1. She can / can't take that class because she can / can't get up at 6:00 am every day!

2. I wanted to attend the session because I can / can't understand American slang very well.

3. I can / can't speak English pretty fluently but I can / can't manage too well in French.

4. She said that she can / can't make it to the meeting tomorrow.

5. I asked her friend to come to the meeting, too. He said that he can.

6. He can / can't pull his weight around here.

7. I can / can't recognize his accent.

8. I can / can't work my fingers to the bone for this.

9. The Professor says he can / can't comment on that.

10. Because of her work schedule, she says that she can / can't work like a dog this week, but she can / can't put in the time over the weekend.

11. I can / can't attend the review session but I think I can / can't make it in time for the refreshments.

Practice these pairs of sentences:

1. I can't get your lunch.

I can get your lunch.

2. I can play the guitar.

I can't play the guitar.

3. I really believe that I can't adjust to the food in this place.

I really believe that I can adjust to the food in the place.

4. The professor says he can't comment on that.
The professor says he can comment on that.
5. She says that she can work like a dog this week.
She says that she can't work like a dog this week.
6. I can attend the review session, but I can't make it in time for the refreshments.
I can't attend the review session, but I can make it in time for the refreshments.

Read this dialogue with a partner.

A: Can you speak any foreign languages?
B: Yes, I can. I can understand and speak English very well. Also, I can speak French, but I can't speak it very fluently yet. Can you?
A: I can read French, but I can't speak it very well. But I can't speak English at all! Maybe you can help me, if you have some extra time?
B: Sure, I definitely can. I can probably give you a hand with your pronunciation and intonation and I can check your essays, too. What do you think?
A: That'd be great. I can't believe you'd be willing to help me for free! Is there anything I can do to help you out in return?
B: Well, are you free tonight? Maybe we can have a drink together? I can't come too early because I have an Econ class. But I can meet you at Harry's Bar, say, anytime after 9:30. Can you make it then?
A: Sure, I can be there at 9:30. Sounds like a plan.

10.5.5 /-ed/ Pronunciation Rules

- *If the word ends in "t" or "d," pronounce the /-ed/ ending as an extra syllable.*
- *If the word ends in a voiceless consonant, pronounce the /-ed/ ending as /t/. Do not add an extra syllable.*
- *If the word ends in a voiced consonant, pronounce the /-ed/ ending as /d/. Do not add an extra syllable.*

1. harmed
2. allowed
3. helped
4. invited
5. visited
6. stretched
7. rubbed
8. wrapped
9. talked
10. attracted
11. spited
12. fibbed
13. flipped
14. fitted

- *The same rules apply for adjectives with the /-ed/ ending.*
1. excited
2. bored

3. tired
4. fascinated
5. amazed
6. wretched
7. unabashed
8. interested
9. pushed
10. blessed
11. energized
12. mind-boggled
13. uplifted
14. exhausted

10.5.6 Reductions

- *In speaking, some unstressed words are reduced. They join with the previous word and the sounds of both words change to make a new blend.*

How are these sentences usually pronounced?

I have to pay my tuition fees.

She has to pay her tuition fees.

I'm going to mail the application directly to you.

I'm going to mail the application directly to you.

I want to pass that exam next week.

She wants to pass that exam next week.

Practice reading these sentences with a partner.

I have to do everything by the book.

He has to do everything by the book.

I'm going to work like a dog.

He's going to work like a dog.

I don't want to jump through hoops for this job.

She doesn't want to jump through hoops for that job.

I have to do the grunt work, even though I don't want to.

She has to do the grunt work, even though she doesn't want to.

I'm not going to slack off on this one, even though I want to.

He's not going to slack off on this one, even though he wants to.

She has to go back to the drawing board, even though she wasn't going to.

I have to go back to the drawing board, even though I didn't want to.

Do you always have to run the show? I'm going to get sick of it really soon!

He always has to run the show, even though everyone's going to get sick of it.

Read this dialogue with a partner.

A: Can I come over tonight for a study break? I really don't want to start working on the finance project yet. I'm going to stress myself out if I do any more on it tonight.

B: Sure! You can always come to my place if you want to have a break. I have to run some errands after dinner, but I'm going to be back around 8 or 8:30. I can't seem to get my errands done during the day. So can you come then?

A: I have to get something to eat anyway, so that'll be perfect. I always need a break around that time. I'm going to run over to the cafő on Broadway, can I pick you up something there? I don't want to arrive empty-handed!

B: Nah. Don't worry about it. You don't have to bring anything, just yourself! And I can fix you something to eat here, if you don't want to spend the money. I heard that you can't use your student discount at that place, unless you want to buy something that is more than 20 dollars.

A: Really? I was just going to get something small, but you're right that it's pretty expensive, even if you want to just grab a quick bite. If I can have a snack at your house, then that would be great.

B: Okay. Then I'll see you around 8:30, right?

A: Right. Thanks a lot.

B: No worries – what are sisters for?

Chapter 11

Cultural Sensitivity & Etiquette

11.1 Overview

Culture can be defined as views and values possessed by people who have common experience and/or similar education. That shared experience may relate to a variety of spheres: Social, Educational, Geographic, Religious, Political, Corporate, etc. Thus, all these factors that influence culture determine expectations, views, and values. Oftentimes culture is the basis for self-identity and community.

We need to be aware of the complicated nature of culture. It takes time, observation, study, reflection, communication and exploration for you to get to know a new culture well. It is a repeated yet progressive process.

An infinite variety of factors affect cultural beliefs and practices.

- The religion practiced, the language spoken, the roles of men and women, what is funny and what is not, the perception of nature, the importance of individual pursuits, the importance of the group and the meaning of gestures are some of the elements that create culture.

- Within education, in fact, within every classroom in a given culture, a different micro culture also dictates levels of formality and prestige accorded students and faculty outside and within the classroom, and student and teacher roles and behaviors.

- Within corporate culture too, there is another infinite set of factors influencing interaction and these may differ from corporation to corporation. How you greet a colleague, how you write and the purpose of that writing, how you present in a meeting, and whether you meet co-workers outside of work reflect some of the ways in which a corporation develops its own mode of interaction within a given broader culture.

Just as culture plays an important role in human relationships and behavior, it also plays an important part in international business. The need to overcome cultural differences becomes more apparent when we consider the unfortunate consequences of neglecting the importance of other cultures:

1) Financial losses
2) Missed chances for beneficial business relationships

3) Awkwardness, embarrassment, or even humiliation
4) Inefficiency and frustrations as a result of miscommunication

11.2 Cross Cultural Communication

Culture is not stagnant; it changes over time. And though culture is such a broad, dynamic term, we can work to understand a corporation's or individual's cultural context better and thus better communicate with them.

(1) **Identify the cultural context.**

  (a) What religious, corporate, socio-economic community are you engaging?

  (b) What does that community value?

  (c) What are those unconscious biases and assumptions?

(2) **Identify cross-cultural differences.**

General Differences

  (a) How do you differ from them? How are you similar to them?

  (b) Do you consider the culture to be economically and culturally conservative or liberal?

  (c) What is a typical family relationship? Do family members stay close all the time and provide financial means for each other? Do parents make key decisions for children? Does extended family exert a strong influence in the decision-making process?

  (d) What is the traditional level of formality in interactions?

  (e) What seems to matter most: individual achievement or group achievement?

  (f) How much cultural diversity or homogeneity exists within a culture?

  (g) Do words have the same meaning? Does, for example, tomorrow mean tomorrow, or next week?

Specific Differences Related to Business

  (h) Does the culture stress developing trust before joint collaboration on specific projects? Is it goal-oriented or relationship-focused?

  (i) How are business presentations and meetings conducted?

  (j) What are the most commonly accepted after-work social events?

  (k) Are there specific male and female roles within business or within the home? For example, are women in upper management positions? Are men often subordinate to women or vice versa?

  (l) Are directors, presidents, or those in upper management to be accorded special respect?

  (m) Are key decisions made by one or a few people behind the scene? Or is it more of a group consensus in public?

Specific Differences Related to Education

  (n) What is the main goal of education? Is it to foster innovation or to reinforce tradition? Does it advocate depth of a chosen major or breadth of both science and literal arts? How much emphasis is given to ethics and values?

(o) Does education confer social status or prestige? Are certain degrees highly coveted? Is there a different benchmark for different genders in the same culture?

(p) What is the typical relationship between teacher and student? What kind of social status and respect are accorded a teacher? How long does such a relationship last? How difficult is it to become a teacher? How permanent is a teaching position at a given school?

(q) What are classroom dynamics? Are there mainly lectures by teachers? Is active student involvement valued or not? Are all students or only certain selected members of the class encouraged to voice their opinions? Do students ask questions in public or in private? Is a challenge from a student to the instructor viewed positively or negatively?

These questions are not intended to be all inclusive. Rather, they represent some often encountered cultural differences. Most of them do not result in absolute answers, but by addressing them, you will become aware of possible areas of misunderstanding between your own culture and the culture with which you are seeking to do business.
In sum, the key factors in cultural differences include:

· Perception of Gender Roles

· Perception of Space

· Perception of Time

· Perception of Success

· Perception of Change/Risk

· Individualism Vs. Collectivism

· Directness Vs. Indirectness

· Emotion Vs. Logic

· Importance of Hierarchies

· Verbal Vs. Non-Verbal Communication Behaviors

· Role of Humor

· Different Ways of Saying "No"

Special Notes on Perception of Space

Research suggests that there are four major zones of personal space which carry meaningful importance in cross-cultural communication. The categorizations below exclude various factors such as availability of the space, the type of settings, the emotion of the surroundings, etc. It also does not factor into the involving nature of culture.

· Intimate zone (for close relationships) - less than 18 inches (about 0.5 meter)

· Personal zone (for friends) - 18 inches to 4 feet (0.5 to 1.2 meters)

· Social zone (for work) - 4 feet to 10-12 feet (1.2 to 3+ meters)

· Public zone (for formal interaction) – 10-12 feet and greater (3+ meters and more)

The diagram below represents a general view of the varying perceptions of personal space among selected countries. The list is not meant to be all inclusive. Rather, it serves only for illustrative purposes.

CLOSE   **DISTANT**

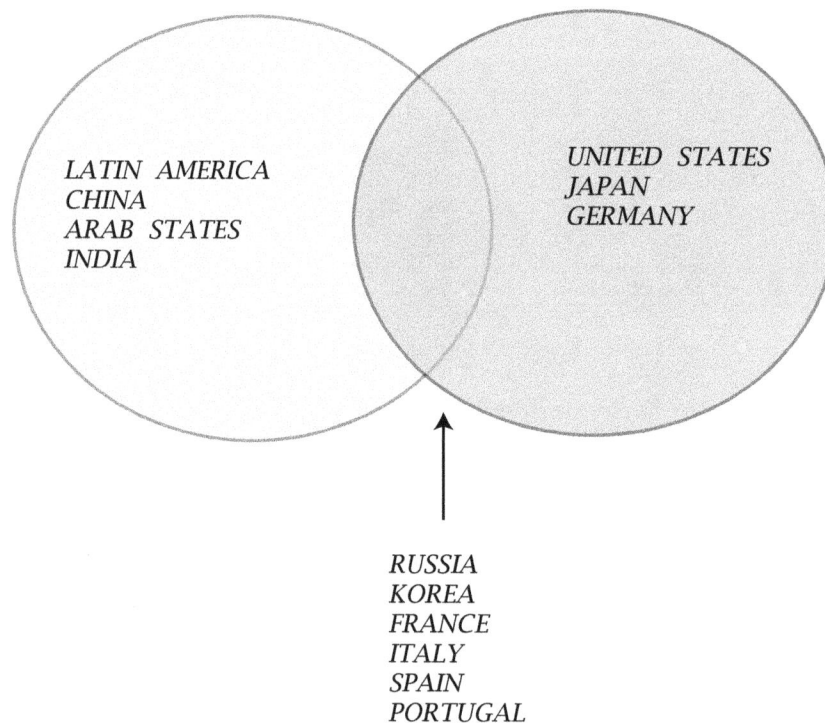

LATIN AMERICA
CHINA
ARAB STATES
INDIA

UNITED STATES
JAPAN
GERMANY

RUSSIA
KOREA
FRANCE
ITALY
SPAIN
PORTUGAL

3. Identify direct and indirect communication styles.

It is generally accepted that Eastern cultures prefer greater indirectness in business engagements than Western Cultures, especially North American and Germanic cultures. In order to identify whether directness or indirectness is favored, it is useful to ask the following:

i Is communication simple and broad or complex and detailed?

ii Does communication involve a clear logic?

iii Is emotion a key factor?

iv What is the degree of informality?

The diagram below provides a preliminary view of the broad cultural tendencies of certain countries.

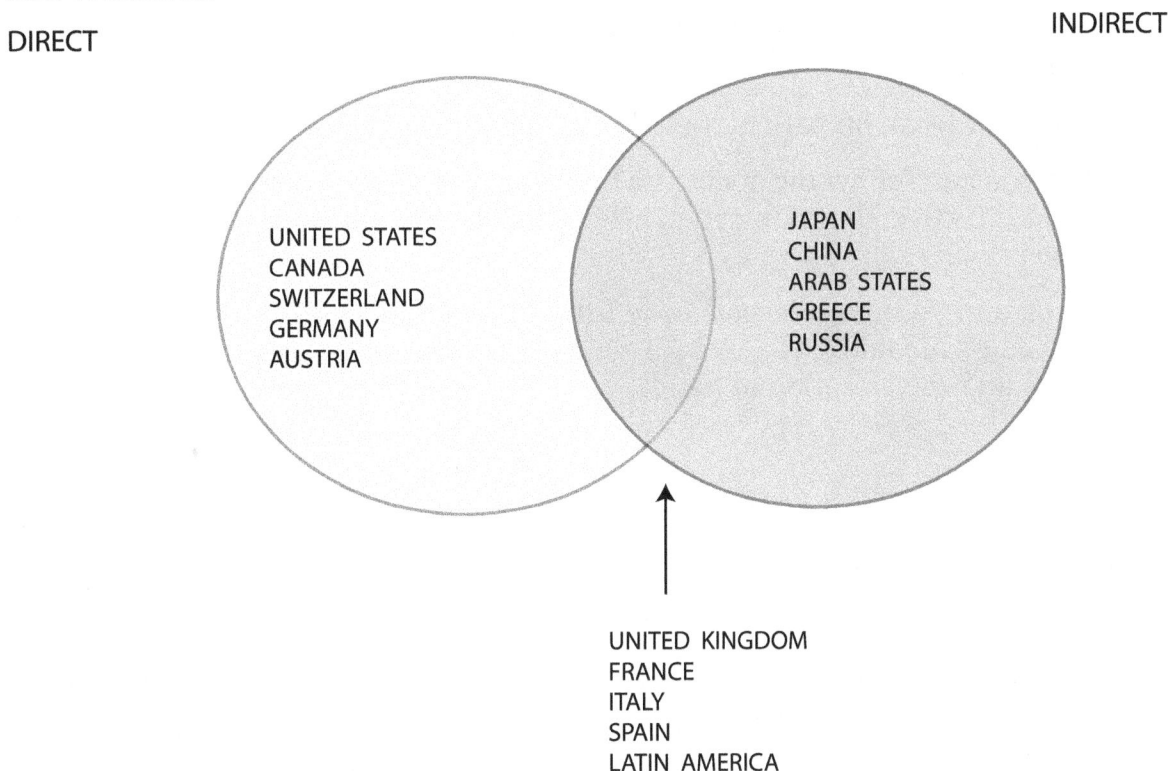

DIRECT   INDIRECT

UNITED STATES
CANADA
SWITZERLAND
GERMANY
AUSTRIA

JAPAN
CHINA
ARAB STATES
GREECE
RUSSIA

UNITED KINGDOM
FRANCE
ITALY
SPAIN
LATIN AMERICA

4. Identify effective communication practices.

(1) When is oral communication appropriate?

(2) When is written communication appropriate?

(3) What is the most popular way to conduct a business presentation?

(4) Is it a constructive or negative approach in facilitating interactions if the objectives are explicitly stated in the beginning?

(5) Other practices include:

- Patterns of reasoning and argumentation
- Level of formality in inter-personal communications

11.3 Tips for Cultural Sensitivity & Etiquette

The most effective means of cross-cultural communication is to stay **open-minded**, **flexible** and **adaptable** to the other culture. That means:

- Avoid ethnocentrism and go beyond stereotypes.

- Always seek common ground.

- Be observant. Pay close attention to non-verbal cues such as facial expression, body language, and reaction from other members of the same group.

- Be diligent. Study your own and other cultures. Study the corporate culture of the company which will interview you or make you a job offer.

- Ask someone you trust about common or most effective practices. Discuss your confusion, doubts or even fears.

- Last but not least, be patient, be tolerant and be accommodating!

Specifically, you can follow the spectrum below to devise your own strategies in achieving the most effective communication when dealing with a different culture within a limited time period.

If **BOTH** you and your counterpart have **little knowledge** of each other's culture, consider using a mediator or a mutual acquaintance with excellent knowledge of both cultures and the situation at hand.

↓

If **you have substantially greater knowledge** about your counterpart's culture, consider accommodating the other's culture practices to reach the most time-effective resolution.

↓

If **you have substantially less knowledge** about your counterpart's culture, consider asking your counterpart to accommodate your cultural practices in the interest of time while you proactively learn about the other culture.

↓

If **BOTH** you and your counterpart have **excellent knowledge** of each other's culture, just improvise and adapt to each other's verbal and non-verbal cues creatively.

Index

www.ingramcontent.com/pod-product-compliance
Lightning Source LLC
Chambersburg PA
CBHW080505110426
42742CB00017B/3001